A HISTORY OF THE

GAA

IN 100 OBJECTS

To Daddy, as a thank you for bringing us to all of those matches around the county and country, now we get to bring you. To Mam, as an apology for all the cursing and roaring you have to tolerate when we're watching matches at home, I hope our family has many more happy GAA memories to come.

A HISTORY OF THE

GAA

IN 100 OBJECTS

Siobhán Doyle

MERRION
PRESS

First published in 2022 by
Merrion Press
10 George's Street
Newbridge
Co. Kildare
Ireland

© Siobhán Doyle, 2022

9781785374258 (Hardback)
9781785374265 (Ebook)

A CIP catalogue record for this book is available from the British Library.

Typeset in Acumin Concept & Garamond Premium Pro by riverdesignbooks.com
Cover design by kvaughan.com

Front cover image: Haughney Memorial Cup. Courtesy of Carlow County Museum and Cumann Lúthchleas Gael Coiste Chontae Ceatharlach.
Back cover image: Waterford Crystal Chandelier. Courtesy of Croke Park Stadium, Dublin.

Merrion Press is a member of Publishing Ireland.

Acknowledgements

This book has been the culmination of many hours of chatting, brainstorming, organising, travelling, researching, writing and editing. There is an enormous amount of people who replied to emails from a stranger, answered phone calls from an unknown number, helped me to connect with others and opened up their collections, their stories and their homes to me. I am grateful to each and every one of them.

I thank Jim Carroll – whose encouragement and enthusiasm has strengthened this project from the very beginning. To my colleagues in the National Museum of Ireland and Technological University Dublin, the support has been greatly appreciated. To Conor Graham, Patrick O'Donoghue, Maeve Convery and Wendy Logue at Merrion Press, thank you for your professionalism and for making the entire process so easy and enjoyable. The abiding contributions of Dónal Hassett, James A. Lundon, Julianne McKeigue, Tomás Rua Ó Cadhla, Joe Ó Muircheartaigh, Connell Vaughan and Jim Whelan have helped enrich the stories that lie within these pages. *Go raibh míle maith agaibh.*

List of Objects

Introduction

In July 1888, a hurling match took place in Con Kearney's field in Carrahan, a townland twelve miles from Ennis, Co. Clare. The prize for the winners was a 5x4 foot banner of green tasselled silk, which is believed to be one of the earliest known GAA trophies. Tulla beat Feakle to win the banner and afterwards, as the Tulla Fife and Drum band led the victorious team through the village, the banner was carried home by the president and vice-president of the club. It remained in the parochial house in Tulla for many years, and today the banner is proudly displayed in Cnoc na Gaoithe, a convent building converted into a cultural and community space that promotes and preserves the traditions and cultures of east Clare. As I walked through the building, I was reminded to tread the floorboards quietly and to speak gently as children's music lessons were taking place, underlining the multi-purpose and busy nature of the building. The banner is kept in a large room that is filled with many historical objects of importance to the local area including trophies, musical instruments and agricultural equipment. As it hangs beside the window that looks out onto Tulla village, viewers' eyes are drawn to the large oil painting in the centre of the banner depicting a hurler in characteristic dress of the time. There is detail on the back of the banner reading 'Won at Carrahan 1888' in large embroidered writing. But the back is not visible to those who walk into the room and see the banner as it is displayed now. To understand the wider historical context of the banner and to recognise its meaning and importance to the community of Tulla, we must look closer; we must read and we must listen to stories. Therein lies the purpose of this book – to gather objects of importance to people and communities across the GAA and use them to get a deeper insight into the evolving meaning of the association.

I realise that the very title of this book – *A History of the GAA in 100 Objects* – is somewhat of a significant claim to make. However, the keyword is *a*. It is *a* history, not *the* history. It does not claim to be definitive. Any book which declares itself to be an official, definitive or authorised history is charged with bias and should be approached with a degree of caution. Furthermore, attempts to capture a definitive history of a given subject are invariably partial and incomplete. This book is no different.

While my aim in developing this book was to be as comprehensive as possible, some gaps remain simply because the objects no longer exist. The origin of the Dingle GAA jersey is an example of a wonderful story of chance and peculiarity, but one that no longer has the original object to give it added weight and power. Jimmy McKenna, a Dingle native and secretary of Dingle football club, was training to be a draper in a shop in Cork city in the 1930s. The Cork county board had ordered a set of red and white jerseys but were displeased with the price of the finished product and returned them to the shop where they were placed in storage. At the time, Dingle had no formal club colours, so Jimmy negotiated a deal with the shop and, by chance, those jerseys became the adopted colours of Dingle GAA club, as

they still are today. These were also Dingle's first professionally made strip, as previous to this each player had their own jersey, usually hand-knitted by their mother. In 1938, Dingle won the county championship wearing those very jerseys, but the historical significance of the jerseys was enhanced the year after, when Kerry faced Meath in the All-Ireland football final. With both county colours being green and gold, Kerry were forced to change their strip. What did they wear instead as they captured the title? You guessed it – the red and white jerseys of Dingle that were rejected by Cork.

Those jerseys, simple in form, weave the threads of a fascinating story that were first sewn in that drapery, became unknotted by the Cork county board and are now forever entangled in the history of Dingle and Kerry GAA. It would have been a lovely addition to include one of those jerseys in this book but such an object is beyond my reach. As I sat in Dingle discussing this story with a politician, a GP and a publican (which I now realise sounds like the start of a bad joke), I was struck by the possibility of things being unintentionally disposed of without realising their historical potential. The original jerseys from 1938 don't need to exist for the story to be legitimate, but it would be nice to have just one of them to compress that story into material form. In many ways, the red and white that Dingle GAA club still wear is a perpetual reminder of that story. Who knows, maybe the Kerry crowd knew well and disposed of all traces that they were the recipients of Cork's sloppy seconds.

Despite those lost objects, the research has been met with a level of openness, warmth and enthusiasm that I could only have imagined. As I approached Lackagh Museum and Heritage Centre in Co. Galway on my first research visit in June 2021, I encountered a small group of people gathered at the entrance. I said to nobody in particular: 'I see by the hurls in your hands that I'm in the right place anyway.' The response, in a strong Galway accent, was, 'No, we're security!' That light-hearted exchange gave me the reassurance I needed that my research would be welcomed with sincerity and fervour, which thankfully continued throughout all of my journeys around the country. The end result is a broad material representation of the major themes that have influenced the development of the association, as well as a glimpse into the technology that has developed rapidly in recent years. Not every significant development appears in this book, nor does every famous match, team or player. Nevertheless, my goal was to present a history of the GAA in an original way that I hope will be enjoyable for history and GAA enthusiasts, wherever they may live.

The GAA's history has never been written through objects, nor have objects been used as the primary form of evidence in a single volume within the context of Irish sport. By examining the GAA in this way, this book is an invitation to view the GAA's history through a new lens, but also to reflect on how much we may not know or how much we may have overlooked. There are a great deal of GAA stories still to be uncovered through objects and I hope there is abundant inspiration here for renewed effort in how we collect and consider our own memories through objects. When objects are considered as representations of the past rather than as evidence to be mined for information or items to be valued for auction, the range of possible objects and ways of viewing them expands considerably. Each object is shaped by a particular context, including matches, historical moments and personal memories. Kilmainham Gaol Museum has in their collection a set of handballs, which are hardly remarkable when described as simply that. But elaborate that the handballs were used by Éamon de Valera (1882–1975) when he was a prisoner in the gaol during the Civil War and those handballs suddenly take on a different historical dimension. Describe how he was thought to have used these to play handball with William Corri, governor of Kilmainham Gaol, and we gain an insight into prison life, how handball was used to break down power dynamics and the importance of sport for internees. The handballs were later thrown over the wall of the prison and collected by the Flewitt family, who lived outside the walls of Kilmainham; they were later donated to the museum. So these handballs, seemingly ordinary at first glance, reveal many layers and stories about different people. It is difficult to understand the history of the GAA and its rules, dynamics and epic encounters without embracing objects like these that help us to narrate the past. The focus of this book is to demonstrate how these objects can develop, represent, reinforce and alter our understanding of the GAA and its history.

A vital task in any new venture is to establish its validity and significance. This book emerged from my own background in history and museum studies, and my abiding interest in the GAA. It is also influenced by my time working in Croke Park as a tour guide, meeting colleagues and visitors to the stadium who dearly love the GAA and make it the successful organisation that it is. This in turn made me insist upon the need to engage with parts of the organisation that go beyond players and champions, on the grounds that only through this expansion would I be able to tell a truly inclusive history of the GAA. Many wonderful people make the GAA special – referees, volunteers, commentators and supporters – and

I have included their stories in this book. Still, I know that many readers will think of objects in their own homes or communities that would merit inclusion as they comb the pages of this book. This is part of the book's purpose – to allow people to think about objects and how we use them as storytelling devices. The evocative power of objects is magnified when people are able to identify a sense of familiarity, recollect their own experiences and see themselves in the stories of these objects. That familiarity may reveal itself by thinking 'we have one of those at home', 'I remember that match' or 'I heard that before alright'. I hope that for many people, the objects' stories bring about a warm sense of familiarity with each turn of the page.

I owe much to the GAA, which has led to many wonderful friendships, strengthened family relationships and built up a spirit of community that has served me well.

My first visit to the GAA Museum was in 1999, when our Bannow–Ballymitty camogie team went on a day trip to Dublin to bookend a successful season after winning the U-14 league and championship. While my teammates competed against each other in the interactive area to determine who could jump the highest or hit the sliotar the fastest, I was in front of a screen with our trainer, Sadie Howlin (1937–2016), watching footage of past All-Ireland finals. Perhaps that sums up my relationship with the

GAA – that I was always much more content observing the game and learning about its past than I ever was playing. Despite this, the championship medal that I won that year is attached to my keys and has been for the last ten years. The front is faded but the engraving on the back is still legible: 'B/B U-14 champions '99'. So I suppose it could be said that I carry my very own GAA object with me every day.

I'm not the only one to have done so. While on a research visit to the Cardinal Tomás Ó Fiaich Library in Armagh in December 2021, I was captured by a particular object when it was placed on my reader's table: an All-Ireland senior camogie medal won by Máire Ní Ghormáin with Antrim in 1945. A pin and clasp was added to the back of the medal with a short chain so that it could be worn as a brooch, which Máire wore every day until she died. I immediately thought of the medal on my keys and also Kathleen Mills' (1923–1996) six All-Ireland camogie medals that she won with Dublin which are fashioned into a bracelet. There in the Ó Fiaich Library, I fortuitously formed an alliance with these women and joined an unspoken club of those of us who have transformed our camogie medals into something beyond GAA memorabilia: objects to wear and use every day. After transforming the medals into keyrings, brooches and bracelets, I think the hope is that they remain

associated with us, the original owners, even when they are circulated amongst other people.

I would return to the GAA Museum many years later as an employee and, in hindsight, the seeds of this book were sown there as I spent many hours perusing the cabinets filled with objects and encountering the extraordinary mix of people who came through the doors. While working front of house in 2014, my colleague and proud Longford man Tommy Flynn was greeting visitors and checking them in for a stadium tour.

'Where are you from?' says Tommy.

'We are from France,' was the reply in broken English.

'Ah right. I'm from Ballymahon meself.'

Cue two very puzzled faces from the French visitors and the rest of us within earshot resigned to knots of laughter at Tommy thinking that Ballymahon would have any resonance to a couple who had just landed in Ireland the day before.

For Tommy and many more, the GAA plays an important role in identity and place, with much to take pride in and celebrate. It contributes to the formation of place identity through diverse social interactions, practices and memories. However, there are many parts of the association that are deeply problematic and there are many injustices that exist within it that should not. I have not set out to expose these issues or to challenge thinking on them, but I do wish to underline that these problems exist, because any history depends on honesty and awareness of the problematic aspects of the past as well as its glories.

It is abundantly clear that the GAA has evolved considerably since its formal establishment in 1884, in ways that connect intimately with major historical developments in Ireland. Its role has been transformed in tandem with significant moments in modern Irish history, such as the War of Independence, mass emigration and the Troubles. Though these historical moments are by no means comprehensively analysed in this book, their inclusion does help in explaining patterns, issues and developments that frame the evolution of the GAA. Not all of the objects stir joyous memories and many are painful reminders of loved ones who are no longer with us. These objects require sensitivity to their multiple meanings, and for the people who hold on to them and their reasons for doing so.

An object that stopped me in my tracks, when conducting research on the material culture of Bloody Sunday for the GAA's centenary programme in 2020, was Annie Burke's glasses, damaged but intact in their leather case. Annie, originally from Co. Sligo, attended the Dublin versus Tipperary challenge match on 21 November 1920, which took a dreadful turn as Crown forces entered Croke Park and opened fire on the thousands of spectators. Fourteen people lost their lives and the events of that day marked a turning point in the War of Independence. Annie herself left Croke Park unscathed, aside from a piece of glass which cut her face. The glasses she wore were damaged by a ricocheting piece of grit and she never wore them again. They were never repaired or cleaned and remained in their case in their disfigured condition. Damaged but not completely broken, the glasses act as a metaphor for all of those who suffered the consequences and traumatic memories of that day in the years that followed. For those of us seeing these glasses 100 years on from when they were last worn by

their owner, they act as an enduring material testimony of the despair of Bloody Sunday and one of the darkest days in the GAA's history.

The research involved in this book has brought me to a variety of locations across the country. It was important that, where possible, I viewed each object myself in person. This meant travelling thousands of miles around Ireland, heavily reliant upon GPS to guide me along many roads that I'll probably never drive again. But each and every journey was worthwhile. In many cases, seeing the object uncovered new information, whether that was noticing marks not perceptible from photo-graphs or a sense of surprise that the objects were not the size I had imagined. It was also useful to get a sense of the environments in which the objects are kept. I absolutely main-tain that it was essential that I spent several hours in the pubs where I sourced some of the objects – purely to familiarise myself with the settings of course. Speaking to the owners of the objects and museum staff who facilitated my research visits was also a useful part of the research process. The casual chats often brought about some interesting and worthwhile anec-dotes. When sitting with Pat Donnellan in Bearna golf club (after arriving twenty minutes late because I stopped off at a hurling match in Athleague, Co. Roscommon and got stuck in a tractor run outside Mountbellew), he spoke about how the standout memory from his many years playing football for Galway was the friendships that he forged with his teammates. Pat also reflected how wherever he was there was football. These reminiscences didn't change how I wrote about Pat's All-Star jersey, nor did it directly add any information to the history of the object itself. But it did make me realise that writing this book is not simply about gathering facts and presenting them; it's about connecting with people and their stories, and using objects to mediate their past ideas, memories and experiences.

The GAA serves different functions and identities in different places, and significant if subtle differences are to be expected. Therefore, not every region could provide object stories for each code, as is desirable. I expanded the research beyond traditional GAA strongholds, with their long lists of achievements, to encompass every county and its own GAA history. Although each county has different strengths and interests within the GAA context, there are shared patterns in collecting objects. If I had filled these pages with match programmes, medals, trophies and jerseys, the research would have been done in a fraction of the time and without me having to travel as far. But while

these objects are valuable in telling stories and are justifiably included in the book, moving beyond them to find a more varied selection was the real task.

One research visit brought me to the home of Paddy Flanagan (1930–2022) in Mullingar, who served in many roles within GAA circles as a player, county board secretary, public relations officer, Leinster Council delegate and president of Westmeath GAA. The meticulously gathered newspaper cuttings, team sheets, notes and scrapbooks in Paddy's personal archive act as a handwritten love letter to Gaelic games. His method of collecting and record-keeping set in motion his initiative to improve the contents and quality of match programmes in Leinster and to transform them into a more meaningful match-day souvenir. There are many more collectors across the country who, like Paddy, have dedicated rooms full of trophies, documents and memorabilia. They form an important community of people who gather and safeguard information that is difficult to find elsewhere.

It has been difficult for me to write a historical account of the GAA without viewing it through my own personal frame of reference. Before I started writing this book, or indeed any other history project I have embarked on to date, I have come to the subject with my own personal bias, sometimes consciously, but more often as a subconscious product of my background. I was brought up in rural Wexford in a busy house where Sundays were technically a family day, but realistically they were dictated by the GAA and what match was on. And that routine still stands. If there's a match in Wexford Park at 2 p.m., the Sunday roast is on the table at the earlier time of 12.30 p.m. No tay, no wash-up, straight out the door. Matches further afield require a more organised routine that involves sandwiches, sucky sweets, flags and headbands – because God forbid some stranger wouldn't know that we were supporting Wexford.

I'm not sure at what age I was brought to my first GAA match, but the first one I remember was the Leinster hurling final between Wexford and Kilkenny in Croke Park in 1997. Billy Byrne came off the bench to score 1–2 that day and helped to secure victory over our biggest rivals, earning him the title of super sub in Wexford hurling folklore forevermore. But in all honesty, my only vivid memory of that day is watching our captain lift the Bob O'Keeffe Cup. I don't know if we travelled by car or by train, I can't recall the pre-match buzz on the walk to the stadium, I can't even remember which Guiney twin was captain that day without double-checking. This demonstrates the selectivity of memory – the memories that we forget and the memories that we hold onto – on the basis of our experience. My memory of that day is absolutely clouded because Wexford won. I doubt that the trophy presentation would be etched in my memory all these years later had Kilkenny emerged victorious. Memory does not function in an organised, linear way. It transforms according to time and progressions. Perhaps I only attached meaning to that moment of victory because it took a while for Wexford to capture it again – six years, eleven months and twenty-one days. Not that I was counting.

By the time we won a Leinster hurling title again in 2004, I was in secondary school and, crucially, a school that lay on the Wexford–Kilkenny border. In many ways, attending a secondary school that comprised half Kilkenny and half Wexford students framed my relationship with the GAA, and hurling in particular. Those boundaries that go between counties allow us to display strong allegiances to GAA teams, provide a focus for intergenerational discussions about 'golden eras', and are a basis for the development of solidarity but also rivalry with others. This model is often intensified at club level; as the boundaries get tighter, the familiarity is deeper and thus more compelling. However, in the GAA context, your biggest rival may ultimately be your ally. A player you may mark or shout against at club level may be someone you play with or support at county level.

I abhor when Wexford lose to Kilkenny. That need to beat Kilkenny begins with hurling, but the competitiveness goes beyond it. If Wexford lost a game of tiddlywinks to Kilkenny on the bridge in New Ross, I'd probably be annoyed for the evening. But truthfully, Kilkenny is home to some of the most pure and kind-hearted people that I know. I'm even fond of some of them I've never met. My grandfather John Lonergan (1899–1968) served in many roles within Kilkenny GAA circles: chairman of the South Kilkenny Board, trainer with Carrickshock, selector with the Kilkenny minors and referee when needs must. He died in 1968 and I know little of him except for Mam's recollections that are only shared when prompted. As far as I know, we have nothing of him. No material possession as a reminder of his presence. We often forget or throw out the things that we cannot bear. He left a young family of five behind and the closest any of his grandchildren have been to him is visiting the gravestone above his narrow bed of clay in the old cemetery in Hugginstown. Yet, without knowing him, I do feel a sense of the man he was through the GAA. The only reason

we even have photographs is because of those taken within the GAA context – usually him standing in a pre-match team photo. Scouring through archives, there are many references to him in the *Kilkenny People* and *Munster Express* newspapers. Chronologically in those archives, he is recorded as chairing meetings, then rising up the ranks of administration in Kilkenny GAA. Next is a notice that he is stepping down as chairman due to illness after fourteen years; the reference following this is a note from his widow and children thanking those who attended his funeral and sympathised with them during their bereavement. But his mentions in the local newspapers didn't stop there. A year after his death, a shield was put up in his memory and was played for in the Kilkenny Southern junior championship. Who knows what became of the shield itself as an object. Maybe it is still proudly displayed on a dresser, maybe it is lying in an attic in a box of unwanted memories, maybe it is waiting to be bought at a car boot sale or maybe it is long gone and used as kindling. Sure those Kilkenny lads are always winning trophies anyway. My point is that not everything is kept and not everything needs to be kept. Objects come and go. Some are treasured, some are intentionally disposed of and some are genuinely lost to the passage of time. Some people leave only light footprints and some leave none at all in terms of material possessions. That's why the things that survive – those crumpled letters, that jersey that's way too small now and the match programme creased from being in the back pocket on the journey home – are special.

This book is organised chronologically by decade, with a short essay contextualising each object by discussing its creation, provenance, purpose and custodian. The evolution in types of objects as the book advances reflects developments in design, technology, politics and society. The first objects presented here explore the GAA before its official establishment as a sporting organisation. Then a number of objects which have been utilised in explanation of the GAA's origins are introduced. With these objects, readers can get a sense of the early years of the GAA. The survival of many of these objects is phenomenal and their historical significance is enormous.

Moving into the late 19th and early 20th centuries, the objects represent some of the ways in which the GAA first operated. One of the enduring challenges of this era is that the objects tend not to be as varied as with other decades. However, the stories that these objects tell are rich and varied. Many of them are paper-based documents, and the voices emerging from the scrawled words are overflowing with startling clarity and purpose. The objects from the 1910s and 1920s are inevitably wrapped up in events of the revolutionary period in Ireland. This was a time of mass violence, death, internment, trauma and intense expressions of nationalism, and the objects reflect this. It also coincided with the GAA becoming more widespread and evolving into a more structured organisation. As for the objects from the 1930s and 1940s, the Irish diaspora has a much louder voice in this section of the book than any other. Many of these objects demonstrate the development of the GAA in different parts of the world. The objects that represent the 1950s until the present day are a broad mix of artworks, ephemera, equipment and memorabilia that reflect how the social and cultural role of the GAA has changed. This part of the book

also focuses on how the GAA has responded to its environment and the impact made by new technology.

Taken individually or as a whole, the 100 objects contained in this book provide a snapshot of the GAA's history; but more than that, they illuminate how the things that we keep both drive and reflect the meanings that we attach to the past. That these objects are included in a book about the material culture of the GAA is very much a collective effort. I hope this book will be the starting point for a new interpretation of GAA history that builds upon the foundations that have been laid by those who have collected, cherished and shared these objects.

100 Objects

1. Wooden Mether (Medieval)

© National Museum of Ireland

When the Liam MacCarthy Cup made its appearance as the trophy presented to the winners of the All-Ireland senior hurling championship, the *Irish Examiner* reported how it 'greatly enhanced the interest manifested in the All-Ireland competition'. The cup was gifted to the GAA in 1922 by Liam MacCarthy (1853–1928), who was a prominent figure in GAA circles in London. It was wrought by Edmund Johnson Jewellers on Grafton Street, Dublin and its design was based upon the form of a four-handled medieval wooden drinking vessel.

Known as a mether, this vessel has a four-sided body with four handles. Methers in various forms have an ancient history as communal wooden drinking vessels. During medieval banquets, they were passed around and guests were expected to drink moderately so that the mether could complete the circuit before the contents were drained. This ritual is also practised in GAA circles when celebrating success with a swig from precious silverware, including the Liam MacCarthy Cup. The tradition is punishable by a twelve-week ban and in 1979, the Leitrim GAA convention suggested that the shape of GAA trophies be changed in order to 'curb the evils of drinking from GAA trophies'.

In medieval times, it was essential that the king's ale contained in methers made a full circuit of the banqueting hall for his honour and legitimacy to be realised. Parading the Liam MacCarthy Cup to as many schools and clubs as possible around the winning county before it is returned each autumn ahead of the senior hurling final is an important task of the All-Ireland champions. The cup can be seen not only as a material prize for reaching the pinnacle of hurling, but as an item of desire to be venerated and enjoyed by all in the community.

2. Hair Hurling Ball (Early 15th century)

© National Museum of Ireland

Hurling descended from ancient stick-and-ball games played in early medieval Ireland but traces of the game prior to the formal establishment of the GAA are limited. This rare example of an early hurling ball has been radiocarbon dated to the time interval between 1402 and 1435. It was found by Hugh Lyons in 1975 while hand-cutting turf in a bog in Lavally, Co. Sligo.

The ball is made from matted cow hair with a plaited horsehair covering, which was used for many folklife objects where durability was required. The cord was wound around the ball in an interlaced way, fully protecting the ball within. Hair hurling balls form part of a long-standing tradition associated with the festival of Bealtaine (1 May). It was the custom during Bealtaine for a newly married couple to decorate a hurling ball with silver or gold lace and tassels. The ball was then hung on the community May bush or given as a gift to an unmarried man. Bealtaine also marked the start of summer hurling and in Kilkenny, women gifted men with new hurling balls on this day.

This hurling ball is one of fourteen in a collection at the National Museum of Ireland, some of which date back to the 12th century. The first one was discovered in Kerry in 1910, with the most recent find coming in Mayo in 2010. All of the balls were found in areas of cut blanket-bog, which ensured the preservation of this valuable evidence of hurling as an ancient phenomenon. These hurling balls are of enormous historical and archaeological significance and illustrate the patterns of evolution in the game of hurling and its equipment.

Castle Blaney

JOHN NIXON D.1818

3. Illustration of Handball Game (1785)

Monaghan County Museum

This illustration is one of the earliest records of handball in Ireland and depicts the game being played against a ruined castle wall. It was painted by John Nixon (*c.*1759–1818), a London-based amateur artist who became best known for his caricatures of urban society. He combined business and pleasure by both trading and sketching on the frequent tours that he made to Ireland in the 1780s and 1790s. It is on one of these trips that Nixon likely created this illustration.

The ruins in the illustration are of Blaney Castle, Co. Monaghan, which was built in 1621 and is the site around which the town of Castleblaney developed. The castle was captured in 1641 and destroyed, eventually disappearing in the 19th century; no trace of it remains today. Its ruins, as depicted by Nixon, show evidence of a three-storey building with high gables, making it an ideal location for the game of handball. Handball was predominantly played in appropriated spaces such as abandoned buildings, hillside lime kilns and ruins, such as those of Blaney Castle. In the town statutes of Galway, written in 1527, the playing of handball and hurling against the walls of the town was forbidden. The document states that 'at no time the use nor occupy the hurling of the little ball with hockey sticks or staves, nor use a handball to play outside the walls, but only the great football on pain of the pains above limited'.

Purpose-built courts first emerged in the late 1700s and typically comprised a wide front wall and two short side walls on either side. The first indoor 40x20 handball court in Ireland was built at Oldtown, Co. Dublin, in 1969 and their designs have since incorporated various combinations of solid walls, viewing windows and raised viewing spaces above.

4. 'Citie of the Tribes' Banner (c.1800s)

GAA Museum, Croke Park

In 2001, this banner was presented to the GAA Museum where it was gratefully accepted by museum staff and the GAA President, Joe McDonagh (1953–2016). Previous to this, it had been in the possession of the Walsh family of College Road in Galway city for generations. John Walsh (1872–1923), a custodian of the banner, represented Galway at intercounty level and captained College Road to its first county championship title in 1892. It is thought that John and his teammates carried the banner through the streets of Galway on one of the most remarkable and significant days in the history of the GAA – Gaelic Sunday. In defiance of the British authorities' attempted crackdown on GAA activities by insisting no matches could take place without prior written permission being sought and granted, the GAA held a match in every parish in Ireland at precisely the same time – 3 p.m. on Sunday, 4 August 1918. Later, this flag was buried in the Walsh family's back garden on College Road for safekeeping from those who

may have viewed the banner as an emblem of that defiance.

The banner is of green poplin and depicts a wolfhound lying at the feet of Hibernia, who carries a shield bearing the crests of the four provinces in her left hand and a pole in her right with 'Citie of the Tribes' written on a narrow flag. The Citie of the Tribes refers to the fourteen merchant families who effectively ran the city of Galway from the 15th to the 17th centuries, playing an important role in its establishment and development by commissioning public and religious buildings and developing trade networks. This scene is against a background of a mountain range with a round tower, Celtic cross, armoury and a book titled *Ireland A Nation* to the right. On the other side of the banner is a galleon ship and a rampant lion which feature on the Galway crest against a maroon background. Above this is 'Gaels na Gaillime' surrounded by a white shamrock motif and below the crest are two hurls and a Gaelic football.

5. Michael Cusack's Blackthorn Stick (*c*.19th century)

GAA Museum, Croke Park

In the late 17th and early 18th centuries, walking sticks became a popular fashion accessory for men. This walking stick belonged to GAA founder Michael Cusack (1847–1906) and has become synonymous with his appearance. This type of walking stick, also known as a shillelagh, is a traditional walking stick of Ireland associated with folklore and given as a symbol of coming of age to young men. Originating from shepherds' walking sticks, they were used as fashion accessories, walking aids and also for self-defence.

This walking stick is made of blackthorn, which is a thorny shrub commonly found in the hedges of rural Ireland. Naturally curved and with a crooked end, ancient hurls would have resembled this type of stick. During the 19th century, walking sticks were viewed as non-verbal symbols of masculinity and the way a man held his walking stick could signal his identity, social status and behavioural tendencies. Visual images of Cusack are scarce, but a studio photograph shows him posing and holding a walking stick in his right hand. The pose, including the walking stick, was used as the basis for a statue of Cusack in Croke Park underneath the stand named in his honour.

This walking stick came into the possession of Wexford man William Foley, who had attended a GAA meeting in Thurles in the early 1900s. After the meeting, a young boy played a prank and pulled the chair Cusack was sitting on from under him. William and his friend Sean Etchingham ran after the culprit and brought him back to apologise to Cusack. As a reward for finding the young boy, Cusack gave his watch to Sean and this walking stick to William.

6. Letter from Michael Cusack to Maurice Davin (1884)

GAA Museum, Croke Park (on loan from Pat Walsh, Carrick-on-Suir)

Michael Cusack had strong cultural and sporting interests and was involved in the Irish language revival movement in the 19th century. Acutely aware of the growing popularity of English sports in Ireland, such as rugby and cricket, he regarded sport as an intrinsic feature of traditional Irish culture and believed that it should be used to promote a distinctive national identity. Cusack's enthusiasm for traditional games was shared by many, but especially by Maurice Davin (1842–1927), an athlete from near Carrick-on-Suir, Co. Tipperary, who had an international reputation. Cusack wrote this letter to him in August 1884 calling for the GAA to be formed before the end of the year.

The contents of the letter give an insight into Cusack's vision for the association. He outlines how his connections with the national press will help garner support and highlights the importance of working together 'caring for none but the Irish people and quietly shoving aside all who would denationalise these people'. Cusack's plans were for the organisation to be nationwide by 1885 and his hope was for national gatherings to be held thereafter. Davin enthusiastically supported these ideas and after this letter, both men set about enlisting the help of others. In October 1884 an article appeared in *The Nation* newspaper calling for the revival of Ireland's national pastimes governed by Irish people.

Cusack insisted that 'the business must be worked from Munster' and that a meeting take place in 'some central place in Tipperary on the 1st of Nov[ember] next'. That central place was Hayes Hotel in Thurles and the GAA was born, as devised by Cusack in this letter.

4 Gardiner's Place
The Gaelic Union

Dublin Aug. 26 - 1884

Dear Mr Davin - The Irish Assoc. with its rules, &c. must be formed before the end of this year. The Assoc. could organise the whole Country within the year 1885. We could then safely hold the projected nat'l gathering in 1886. The business must be worked from Munster. Suppose we held a meeting of delegates in some central place in Tipperary on the 1st of Nov next?

Don't bother your head about Dublin. The place couldn't well be worse than it is. Will have to look

to the provinces for men. Dublin will have to fall in or keep up the connection with England.

I have written to Cork this day telling them that you have responded most heartily. I am sure Mr Stack of Listowel will look after north Kerry. Although I am not a member of the Nat'l League, I think I am not without influence with several of the leading members. The Nat'l press will give me room for squibs when I am ready. The Shamrock is also at my disposal. I hope to see it

enlarged in about a month and then the education of the people could start in earnest. The paragraphs on athletics in United Ireland are exploding like shells in the enemy's ranks. Of course they know it is my doing and that therefore the paper is not likely to change for soon.

I have found it to be utterly hopeless to revive our nat'l pastimes without the assistance of the leaders of the people; and I have not hesitated to urge my claim with a persistency that

brooks no refusal. After a protracted struggle I won all round. Our business now is to work together caring for none but the Irish people, and quietly shoving aside all who would denationalize the people.

I'll write to you again when business is a little further advanced.

With many thanks
I am
Yours faithfully
Michael Cusack

Maurice Davin Esq.

7. Bray Emmets Banner (1887)

Bray Emmets GAA Club

Believed to be one of the earliest known GAA banners, this poplin banner represents the Bray Emmets club which was founded in 1885. The painted banner has a portrait of Robert Emmet (1778–1803) in an oval centrepiece surrounded by ornamental work in embroidery. It was commissioned by the club in 1887 and was designed by artist W.J. O'Grady, who established his practice as a banner maker in Dublin in 1875.

The club started its GAA life in Wicklow but moved to play in the Dublin championship soon after. In 1902, the club represented Dublin to win the All-Ireland football final and later returned to the Wicklow championship. Bray Emmets are named in honour of rebel leader and orator Robert Emmet. Although Emmet had no particular affiliation with Bray, it was commonplace for clubs to direct their nationalism into club names and memorialise patriotic figures in this way. This is especially evident in overseas GAA clubs, such as Sean McDermotts (Birmingham), Edmonton Wolfe Tones (Canada) and Pádraig Pearse GAA Club (Chicago).

The banner has been present at many commemorative events for Robert Emmet, including the centenary of his death in 1903 when 80,000 people marched the streets of Dublin. For many years, it took pride of place in the Bray Emmets clubhouse where it was always well admired. In 1970, it was presented to the GAA for safekeeping by Bray Emmets President Matt Britton. The presentation was made at the Scór final in Liberty Hall, where GAA President Séamus Ó Riain (1916–2007) accepted it on behalf of the association. The banner was refurbished by nuns in a convent in Nenagh and later by a professional textile conservator. It has changed hands on many occasions, but the conscious intention of its custodians has always been to protect the banner and its historical significance.

8. Davitt and Croke Commemorative Plate (*c.*1888)

Michael Davitt Museum, Straide

Michael Davitt (1846–1906), born in Straide, Co. Mayo, had a rich and varied career: Fenian, politician, author and international humanitarian. He was a founder of the Land League, a powerful political organisation whose goal was to assist the tenant farmer and stop evictions, reduce rents and ultimately enable farmers to own the land they worked on. A friend of Michael Cusack, Davitt was consulted in advance of the foundation of the GAA in 1884 and he concurred with the aims and ethos of the association.

Davitt's involvement with the GAA was practical and generous. He wrote the preface for the GAA rule book in 1888, publicised GAA activities in a weekly newspaper he edited in London called *The Labour World* and also contributed financially. Davitt is depicted on this commemorative plate along with fellow founding patron of the GAA, Archbishop Thomas Croke, who was also a champion of the Land League. The handshake underneath

their portraits perhaps represents the significant contributions both men made to the GAA in 1888, the year that this plate was manufactured. In this year, Davitt financially bailed the association out of financial difficulty after a failed tour of the United States, and Croke played an influencing role in reconciling factions emerging internally within the GAA.

A vast amount of decorative tableware was produced in the United Kingdom for export during this period. These plates appealed to consumers not just as functional tableware but as works of art and items of visual and historical interest. The portraits are printed in sepia between sprays of shamrock painted green, and the patterns present distinct Celtic symbols, including the figure of Hibernia in the centre. This plate is part of a thirty-two-piece tea set by Skelson and Plant that depicts key figures in 19th-century Ireland including John Dillon, William E. Gladstone, William O'Brien and Charles Stewart Parnell.

29

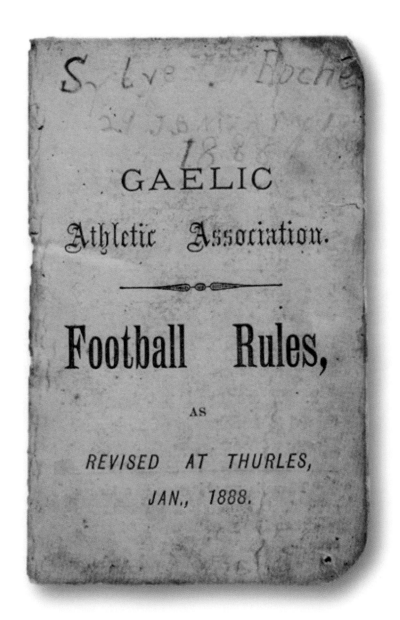

9. GAA Rule Book (1888)

Image by Noel Campbell © National Museum of Ireland

In the early years of the GAA, Gaelic games were mainly local events with considerable variation in how the sport was played in different pockets of the country. This resulted in many games being abandoned due to opposing teams playing under different rules and unable, or unwilling, to adjust their play in accordance with the play of their opponents. The GAA was anxious to standardise the rules and structure of its games, and in 1885, as the first president of the association, Maurice Davin drafted the early rules for Gaelic games. In 1888, this rule book was published outlining a set of rules for Gaelic football. These included guidelines for the size of the playing field, the use of goalposts and regulations for throw-in, which stipulated that each team must stand in two ranks opposite each other in the middle of the field, each holding the hand of their opponent.

This rule book, with the front cover missing, belonged to Sylvester Roche from Drogheda, Co. Louth, who signed his name and the date (29 January 1888) on the first page in pencil. It comprises thirteen rules; by 1896, there were twenty-seven rules, with each new rule book replacing previous versions. The rules were communicated via these printed books, which cost one penny, and were also published in newspapers. Teams gradually adjusted their accustomed tradition of play in accordance with these rules, but their implementation was slack at first. In 1890, owing to several accidents during matches, the Carlow Gaelic Club vowed to carry out Rule 13, which prohibited players from wearing boots with nails or iron tips. The rules of the game have continued to develop as necessitated by advancement in skills, physicality and tactics, and have been subject to much change, debate and controversy.

10. Handball signed by Fr Tom Jones (*c.*1890s)

Kerry County Museum

Fr Tom Jones (1868–1950) had a strong reputation in handball circles, being considered 'the greatest handball player Ireland has ever produced'. In 1886, at the age of eighteen, he was the handball champion of Ireland and many of the older generation claimed that he would have had a long and outstanding career in sport were it not for the fact that he put his religious vocation before everything else. At the time, handball was a professional sport and Fr Jones was forced to retire from competitions due to his ordination to the priesthood in 1896. This is one of the handballs that he played with and is signed with well-worn signatures, presumably of his fellow handball players.

On 26 April 1916, Fr Jones saved the lives of eight seamen when a Norwegian boat, the *Carmanian*, was targeted and sunk by a German submarine off the Kerry coast. The crew was set adrift in two lifeboats – one landed safely, but the other drifted for almost fifty hours before coming close to the cliff at Ard na Caithne at Baile na bPoc in the Kerry Gaeltacht. Fr Jones took charge of rescue operations, fastened a rope around his body and carried the crew to safety one by one, with the help of local men Pat Lynch, Pat O'Connor and Pat James O'Connor. Undoubtedly, the strength and fitness needed to carry out this act of bravery came from Fr Jones's many years spent on the handball court.

Handball played a significant role throughout Fr Jones's life. In 1946, he founded Glenbeigh handball club and it was decided to name the new court the Fr Jones Memorial Court. His imprint is still seen today in the handball community of Co. Kerry, with the Fitzgerald/Jones handball club he founded in Tralee in 1949, alongside his former doubles partner John Fitzgerald, still in existence.

11. Tubberdora Cap (*c.*1890s)

Lár na Páirce, Thurles

In the early years of the GAA, one of the most successful club teams was Tubberdora. From the parish of Boherlahan/Dualla, they captured three All-Ireland hurling titles representing Tipperary in 1895, 1896 and 1898. Their playing gear included a long-sleeved jersey, sash, long trousers and this cap with a blue ribbon at the front. The cap is lined with cotton and has 'T.H.C.' embroidered in gold lettering, which stands for Tubberdora Hurling Club. This cap is of a similar style to those that are presented to individuals or teams to mark a special occasion or reward an achievement in sports including rugby and soccer. However, those are more ornamental caps and it is less common for them to be worn on the playing field. These same Tubberdora caps of the 1890s were also worn when Tipperary won the All-Ireland hurling title in 1916.

Tubberdora's win over Navan Pierce Mahonys from Co. Meath in the 1895 hurling final was followed by controversy. Two days after the final, a letter appeared in the national papers from referee J.J. Kenny, who stated that he incorrectly awarded Tubberdora a point. He admitted that Tubberdora scored a point from outside the 21-yard line, which was illegal at the time, but he awarded it nonetheless. Consequently, the correct scoreline should have been a draw. Navan Pierce Mahonys did not press the issue any further and the Central Council presented them with a special set of medals inscribed 'Virtual Champions of Ireland 1895'. Tubberdora's win the following year in 1896 was the first All-Ireland final held in the grounds of what is now known as Croke Park.

12. Aghabullogue Hurl (1890)

Kilmurry Independence Museum

This hurl was used during one of the first All-Ireland hurling finals, which was played on 16 November 1890 in Clonturk Park, close to Croke Park. With no specifications for the design and shape of a hurl, this one is typical of the period, with a narrow bas, almost like a hockey or shinty stick. The hurl was used by one of the Aghabullogue players who represented Cork in the final versus Wexford's Castlebridge.

The teams, which were 21-a-side, played the game in their bare feet. This was perhaps to blame for Aghabullogue's Tim O'Connor having his toe broken, one of many incidents during the game. In fact, it was Castlebridge's 'undue roughness' that led to Aghabullogue captain Dan Lane, in agreement with the referee, withdrawing his team. At that time, a goal exceeded any number of points in value and Castlebridge were leading 2–2 to 1–6 before the match was abandoned. The matter was considered at the next meeting of the Central Council and on hearing referee John Sheehy's report, it was recommended that the game be awarded to Cork. Aghabullogue were declared All-Ireland champions by a single vote.

The turn of the century marked the end of Aghabullogue as a force in Cork senior hurling, but it would not see the end of hurling achievements for members of the 1890 team. The following year, a new rule allowing county champions to select top players from other clubs for intercounty games was introduced and many Aghabullogue members were part of the Redmonds' club success. In 1901, Redmonds represented Cork in the All-Ireland hurling final versus London. Although Redmonds lost the final, there was still a strong Aghabullogue connection, with Dinny 'Stonewall' Horgan and his brother Michael on the victorious London team.

13. All-Ireland Football Challenge Cup (1896)

Tony Honan Antiques, Ennis

The All-Ireland Football Challenge Cup was the first cup used for the All-Ireland football championship. It was presented to the GAA on 18 July 1896 by Archbishop Thomas Croke, patron of the association, who also donated an identical cup for the hurling championship at the same time. A rule is now in place which prohibits trophies being named after a living person, so such a tribute could not be accepted today.

The cup is replete with Irish symbols, the four provincial crests and an engraving of Archbishop Croke's portrait. The hurling cup has a narrow stem and stand; this cup had the same form, but was damaged sometime throughout the years. The winners of the cup are engraved on the back, with the first winners, Young Irelands club in Dublin, claiming it in 1896, Ballina Stephenites winning it three times consecutively from 1907 to 1909, and Lees of Cork the last winners in 1913. It was not customary to present cups to the winners on the day of the final, as is now a familiar sight on All-Ireland final days. Instead, a representative from the GAA Central Council, usually the president or secretary, would travel to the winning county at a later date to formally present the cup and medals.

The cup lay dormant for a long period of time and, with its historical significance unbeknownst to its owner, was used as a flowerpot for many years. It was rescued from obscurity by Tony Honan, an antique shop owner in Ennis, Co. Clare, who often displays the cup in the shop window on Main Street ahead of big match days in the nearby county grounds of Cusack Park.

14. Archbishop Croke Stained-glass Window (early 1900s)

Cathedral of the Assumption, Thurles

Thomas Croke (1823–1902), Catholic Archbishop of Cashel and first patron of the GAA, devoted much energy to the GAA from its inauguration. Archbishop Croke mixed his nationalistic views with religious teachings and he used his position to publicly support campaigns such as the Land League and Home Rule. He played a multifaceted role in the history of his times as a religious leader, Irish patriot and defender of his people.

The stained-glass window in the Cathedral of the Assumption in Thurles, Co. Tipperary, features Archbishop Croke's head on the body of St Thomas Aquinas (1224–1274), the patron saint of Catholic universities, colleges and schools. The cathedral, which is a twenty-minute walk from Semple Stadium, stands on the site of a medieval Carmelite priory and forms part of a group of ecclesiastical buildings on Cathedral Street. Archbishop Croke has many connections with the building itself.

He consecrated it in 1879 and he presented the clock tower to the people of Thurles on the occasion of his silver jubilee in 1895. Archbishop Croke's funeral took place in the cathedral in July 1902 and after Mass, a procession was formed and the cortege made a circuit of the town. It then returned to the cathedral and his remains were laid to rest in a vault at the left-hand side of the altar, in what is now the mortuary chapel.

Archbishop Croke's memory is honoured in many ways across the GAA, with numerous tournaments and trophies named after him, as well as the GAA's principal sportsground, Croke Park, named in his honour since 1913. The stained-glass window, a different form of tribute, is less visible to the public, being situated in the apse behind the altar alongside twenty other decorative windows portraying saints and figures from the Bible.

SANCTVS:THOMAS:AQV

SVMMA
TOTIVS
THEO-
LOGIAE
RIPAR

PRAY·FOR·MOST·D·CROKE ARCHBISHOP·OF·CASHEL

15. Illustration of Gaelic Footballer by George Fagan (*c*.1900s)

This drawing of a Gaelic footballer has been in circulation since the early 1900s. It depicts a footballer in a striking and heroic pose, wearing the shorts, socks, boots and long-sleeved jersey that are typical of the time. The illustration is by artist George Fagan (1879–1907), who was involved in illustrating and writing the earliest Irish-language children's books. The illustration was from the 'Republican Art Series' printed by *The Gaelic Press*, which also included Fagan's depiction of a hurler ready to strike a sliotar mid-air.

The Gaelic Press was a newspaper for the nationalist community owned by Joe Stanley, who oversaw the printing of documents on behalf of the leaders of the 1916 Rising during Easter week. After the Rising, Stanley was one of 1,800 Irish prisoners interned in Frongoch Camp and he became involved in the organisation of Gaelic games there. He wrote a report of a unique football match between Kerry and Louth which became known as the 'All-Ireland behind barbed wire'. This was published in July 1916 in his newspaper *The Gaelic Athlete*, as well as in other Irish newspapers.

Fagan died prematurely in 1907 and his illustrations of the hurler and Gaelic footballer were reprinted and reused on many occasions. An exact date for the illustrations is unknown, but it is prior to 1903, when this image featured on the front page of *The Champion* – a newspaper that advocated Gaelic games. It also featured on the front of the official match programmes for All-Ireland football finals in 1913 and 1914. An edited and digitised version of both of these drawings appeared on the front covers of the All-Ireland final match programmes in 2019, demonstrating how Fagan's illustrations have endured as iconic visual representations of Gaelic games.

16. Map of Croke Park (1913)

GAA Museum, Croke Park

In 1908, Frank Brazil Dineen (1862–1916) from Ballylanders, Co. Limerick, used his own money to purchase the City and Suburban Sports Ground at Jones' Road for £3,250 because the GAA at the time could not afford it. His motivation for buying the fourteen-acre site, which included two houses (Albert Villas), was to 'prevent it falling into less sympathetic hands'. After making restorations to the ground, building terraces and re-laying the pitch, Dineen sold the land to the GAA on 18 December 1913. This map is part of the eleven-page deeds of assignment document, which transferred ownership of the land that shortly afterwards became known as Croke Memorial Park.

The area in red on the map shows the land which was covered by the purchase. The blue area marked 'Belvedere Grounds' relates to land that Dineen was forced to sell to the Jesuit Priests of the nearby Belvedere College when he ran into financial difficulties in 1910. The GAA eventually re-purchased this land, as well as other plots in the vicinity when opportunities arose.

The decision to purchase the grounds at Jones' Road was agreed by a vote of eight to seven at a quarterly meeting of the Central Council in October 1913. This proved a momentous decision, resulting in the venue becoming the GAA's national stadium and administrative headquarters. This map is over 100 years old, so there have been many adjustments to its original plans ever since, but it was Dineen's foresight that laid the foundations for what has become a world-class sports venue.

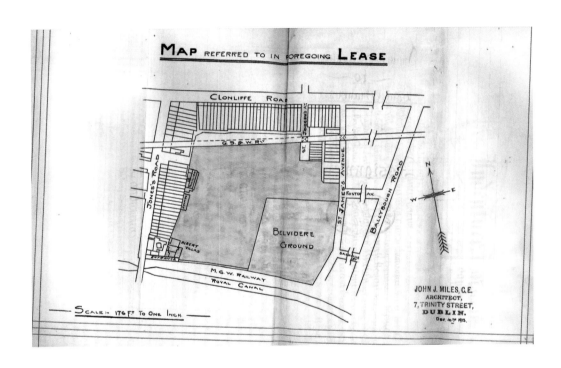

MAP REFERRED TO IN FOREGOING LEASE

CLONLIFFE ROAD

G.S.&W.RY

JONES'S ROAD

ST. JOSEPH'S TCE

ST. JAMES'S AVENUE

FOSTER AV.

BALLYBOUGH ROAD

ALBERT VILLAS

ENTRANCE

BELVIDERE GROUND

M.G.W. RAILWAY
ROYAL CANAL

N
W — E

SCALE:- 176 FT TO ONE INCH

JOHN J. MILES, C.E.
ARCHITECT,
7, TRINITY STREET,
DUBLIN.
DEC. 10TH 1915.

45

Committee Meeting   15th April 1913

15/4/13

The weekly meeting of the County Dublin
Committee was held at 68 Upper O'Connell
street last night, Mr. H. Boland, Chairman,
presiding. There were also present—Messrs.
G. Byrne, F. W. Cooney, M. J. Collins, P. J.
Corbett, W. Crawford, J. Farrelly, A. C.
Harty, J. H. Kenny (for J. Hensey), P. Kena-
fick, J. W. Kenny, J. Kirwan, M. Little, R.
Manifold, H. Morris, T. Murphy, J. M.
O'Duffy, T. Quane, J. Quigley, T. Smyth,
and D. J. Burke, M.A., assistant secretary
and registrar.

REFEREE'S REPORTS.

As a result of referees' reports of matches
played last Sunday Erin's Hope (Junior hurling) and Keatings (Senior football) were declared winners of their respective ties.

FIXTURES.

The following arrangements were made in
connection with next Sunday's matches at
Jones's road:—
Senior Hurling Semi-Final—Kickhams v.
Faughs, 11.45. P. Kenedick.
Junior Football—Rossas v. Crokes 1 p.m.
Referee, Mr. M. J. Collins. Officials—Messrs.
J. Quigley, A. C. Harty, J. Kirwan, J. M.
Duffy, M. Little, J. W. Kenny, and T.
Murphy.
At Ballyboden—
Minor Football—Dundrum Volunteers v.
Fintan Lalors, 12 o'clock. Mr. G. Byrne.

APRIL 27th.

At Jones's road—
Senior Hurling Semi-Final—Davis v. Com-
mercials.
Senior Football Semi-Final—Kickhams v.
Keatings.
Junior Football Semi-Final—St. Patricks v.
Rossas or Crokes.

APPEALS.

The secretary of the Leinster Council in-
timated that an appeal had been lodged by
Dundrum Volunteers against the County
Board's decision in upholding the Bray
Emmets' objection to the Volunteers' team
in the recent Junior Championship tie. The
match, Round Towers v. Bray Emmets, fixed
for next Sunday, had accordingly to be post-
poned pending the hearing of the appeal.
The Hurling League have also appealed
against the County Committee's decision di-
recting the re-fixing of the Rathmines recent
Second Division tie.

BALLYBODEN TOURNAMENT.

Ballyboden Wanderers received a provisional
permit for holding a medal tournament between eight clubs commencing on the 4th
May.

COUNTY COLOURS.

After some discussion it was decided to
adopt as the county colours a light blue
jersey with a white shield, bearing the city
arms, and the assistant secretary was directed
to register same with the Leinster and Central
Councils, and to procure quotations for the
supply of two sets of jerseys.

OVERAGE MINOR PLAYERS.

As the result of the Committee's investigations it was ascertained that Ballyboden
Wanderers and Emeralds had played overage
players in their recent championship tie, and
both teams were accordingly ruled out of the
competition.

REINSTATEMENT.

It was decided to recommend the Leinster
Council to reinstate J. J. Tobin, who had
suspended himself by playing foreign games.

GENERAL.

An application from Fontenoy H.C. for
permission to play a friendly match with
Rathnew H.C. at Rathnew on the 27th inst.
was recommended to the Leinster Council for
sanction. A communication from the Commercial H.C., asking for the re-opening of the
case of a recent transfer from the club, was
ruled out of order.

G.S. & W.R. H.C. applied for the reinstatement
of James Flood who played Association F.C.
on 1st Jany. 1913 but same was ruled out
of order.

Mr Byrnes wrote that he was unable to
attend meeting regarding recent incident in
Blackhall Place. Some members stated that
on making inquiries they had ascertained that
nothing serious had occurred + it was decided
therefore to let the matter drop.

The tournament fee was lodged + the
permit was granted on condition that the
medals or their value be lodged with Committee
one week before date of match — matches to be
played 4 & 11th May + the dates to be arranged
late.

It was decided to invite quotations from
the Blackrock Knitting Co, North William St, Gleesons,
Whelans, Crottys, Elverys + F.G. Hoods — jerseys
to be of Irish wool + preferably of Dublin manufacture

John Tully (Ballyboden) admitted being
overage, + Emeralds wrote that B Donnelly had
admitted being overage.

James McDonald (Kickhams) attended +
stated that the Kilkenny Championship match he
played was in the 1912 championships + took place
in Feb. last. It was unanimously decided to
reinstate Mr McDonald.

H Boland. April 22nd 1913

17. Dublin County Board Minutes (1913)

GAA Museum, Croke Park

On 15 April 1913, the Dublin county board met at 68 Upper O'Connell Street to discuss a number of items on the weekly agenda. This included fixtures, appeals, referee's reports and the disqualification of the Ballyboden Wanderers and Emerald teams for fielding overage players in the minor competition. It was at this meeting that it was decided to adopt the Dublin county colours – a light blue jersey with a white shield bearing the city arms. This decision came one month after the GAA Congress unanimously passed a motion: 'That all counties be required to register county colours with Central Council and no two counties shall be allowed to register the same colours.'

The committee proposed to invite quotations from textile manufacturers to produce the jerseys from Irish wool. Like many jersey designs of the time, they were long-sleeved with high necks or laced collars. The Dublin teams initially wore white shorts, but later changed to navy-blue.

While Dublin consciously chose their county colours, many teams got their colours by chance. During the All-Ireland hurling championship of 1919, the Cork county board offices were raided by Crown forces and the team jerseys – which were then blue with a large gold 'C' on the front – were seized, among other things. At short notice, the Cork county board were forced to borrow a set of red jerseys from the Fr O'Leary Temperance Association team, which was recently defunct after a merger with St Finbarr's GAA club in the city. Red and white then became the official county colours of Cork.

18. Dick Fitzgerald's Coaching Manual (1914)

© National Museum of Ireland

Widely regarded as the first illustrated coaching manual, this book was written by Dick Fitzgerald (1886–1930), who was a holder of five All-Ireland medals with the Kerry footballers. Fitzgerald was well positioned to write this seminal manual, not only because of his exceptional skills as a footballer, but also because he served as an intercounty coach and referee in addition to various administrative roles on club and county committees. His football career was disrupted by his involvement in the Irish revolution, and in 1916 he was interned at Frongoch Camp.

How to Play Gaelic Football retailed at one shilling and was recognised at the time as the authority on Gaelic football instruction and training. The contents include an introductory chapter, sections on the duties of the various positions on the field, an outline of the role of the team captain and referee, as well as guide-lines on applying football methods to hurling. Thomas Barker, photographer with *The Cork Examiner* and a friend of Fitzgerald, provided the illustrations, which include photographs of the footballer demonstrating various skills and fielding positions. Fitzgerald character-ised a transformation in how the sport was understood by the Irish people and this book is a lasting vestige of his innovation both on and off the field.

The book was written while Fitzgerald was still playing as Kerry captain and remained the only published book on GAA coaching until 1958, when fellow Dr Crokes clubman Eamonn O'Sullivan published *The Art and Science of Gaelic Football*. Dick Fitzgerald's legacy lives on in the rich traditions of Kerry football, with the county's home venue in Killarney named Fitzgerald Stadium in his honour.

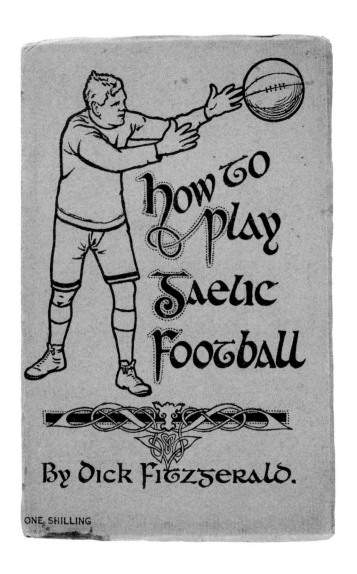

how to
play
Gaelic
Football

By Dick Fitzgerald.

ONE SHILLING

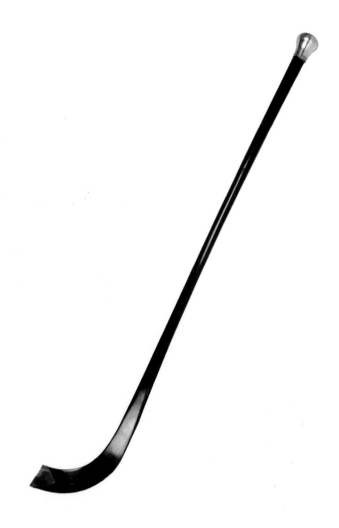

19. Silver Mounted Camán (1914)

Highland Folk Museum, High Life Highland

The origins of shinty (also known as camanachd) are disputed, with some sources contending it originated from hurling and was brought across the sea to Scotland around 2,000 years ago, along with Christianity and the Gaelic language. Others believe its origins come from training warriors or from the chaotic mass games between Scottish Highland clans in the 17th century. Regardless, its crossovers with hurling are unquestionable and the Camanachd Association takes the same community-based approach as GAA clubs.

The Camanachd Cup final is the biggest event in the shinty season and has been running since 1896. It is tradition that the captain of the winning team is given a silver-mounted camán. This camán was presented to William MacGillivray, who captained the Kingussie team in their victory in April 1914. It was the last time the Camanachd Cup was played until 1920, due to the outbreak of the First World War. William enlisted with the Cameron Highlanders along with many members from shinty-playing communities in the Scottish Highlands. Shinty was a way to relax and to switch off from the horrors of war for those stationed in France, with camáns and balls sent from home.

William was killed in action on 18 May 1915 at Festubert in France, which was one of the earliest and most devastating battles of the First World War. William's teammate John Macpherson died on 27 May from injuries sustained in the same battle. In 2014, the Kingussie team reached the Camanachd Cup final and wore jerseys embroidered with the names of the team players from 1914. The team were victorious, beating Glenurquhart 4–0 in Bught Park, Inverness. Separated by 100 years, another winning captain's silver mounted camán made it back to Kingussie.

20. Letter from Bob O'Keeffe to John J. Higgins (1914)

GAA Museum, Croke Park

This letter was written in December 1914 by Robert 'Bob' O'Keeffe (1880–1949), a hurler on the Laois senior team. Addressed to the secretary of the county board, John J. Higgins, the success of the training fund, the forthcoming hurling league and plans to garner success within the county are discussed. In writing, 'Between wet weather and Volunteers the hurling is going to the wall', he is referring to the unfolding political situation in Ireland and how the rise in membership of the Irish Volunteers was affecting hurling in the county.

During the 1914 championship season, Laois won their first Leinster title but lost to Clare in the All-Ireland final in October. O'Keeffe writes how he hopes to capitalise on that success by getting 'into line soon' and making 'a bigger bid for honours in 1915'. These intentions were realised as Laois (represented by Ballygeehan) won their first All-Ireland senior hurling title, with O'Keeffe captaining the team.

After the win in 1915, O'Keeffe wrote another letter to Higgins stating how the win 'affords me the greatest satisfaction too after my 18 years on the hurling field and especially as I feel that my own exertions early last year had a lot to do with Sunday's victory'. There was much praise for O'Keeffe after the 1915 final and GAA Secretary Frank Brazil Dineen commented how 'His [O'Keeffe's] hair has turned grey at the game for he has been over twenty years behind the camán.'

O'Keeffe made his name within GAA circles not only as a player, but as a referee and administrator, holding the posts of treasurer and chairman of the Leinster Council before serving as president of the Association from 1935 to 1938. In 1950, the Leinster senior hurling championship trophy was named in his honour, and although the trophy itself has since been replaced due to wear and tear, it continues to bear Bob O'Keeffe's name.

Borris - in Ossory
18 - 12 - '14

My Dear Higgins,

Your letter &
enclosures to hand
alright. I am pleased
indeed to hear that
the training fund
is such a success.
I spoke to a few lads
from Skeirke & also
wrote them, so I
suppose they won't
forward anything
when they have not
now done so.

We must make a
real effort to start
the Hurling League
immediately after the
Convention. Our lads
are dying on the game
lately. Between wet
weather & volunteers
the hurling is going
to the wall. However
we must get into line
soon as I would not
like to lose Champ.

for this year anyway,
as I intend making
a bigger bid for
honours in 1915. I
am sure there will
be a few good lads
available from the
Juniors.

Best wishes for
a happy Xmas & a
successful G. a. a. year.

Yours Sincerely,
R. O'Keeffe

21. GAA of USA Medal (1915)

GAA Museum, Croke Park

Gaelic games have been played in the USA since the late 1700s and in 1914, the GAA of USA association was formed to co-ordinate games in New York at a time when the games were thriving in the city. Previous to this, GAA in New York was largely organised by individual county associations, with no governing body overseeing the games.

This is a winner's medal from the first GAA of USA football championship in 1915. It is made of solid gold and on the back is engraved 'A. Reilly', who played on the victorious New York Cavan team. The medal features the star-spangled banner and the acknowledged flag of nationalist Ireland at the time – a golden harp on a green background. After the first championship was played in 1915, Gaelic games in New York grew steadily despite two world wars and an economic depression.

Insights into GAA matches and tournaments overseas such as the GAA of USA championship are somewhat limited as results were not always communicated or published in public platforms in Ireland. When a Kilkenny football team beat a Cork selection in a contest in New York in 1909, the result was sent by cablegram to the *Kilkenny People* newspaper offices. The communication channels between the GAA in Ireland and the USA have since expanded and indeed the status of New York GAA has been endorsed by their inclusion in the Connacht senior football championship in 1999. Camogie has been played in New York since the 1960s, and in 1996, hurling in New York was given a notable boost when they won the All-Ireland senior B hurling championship, beating Derry in the final.

22. Poster Banning GAA Events (1916)

Military Archives, Rathmines

1916 was a pivotal year in the creation of the modern Irish state. On Easter Monday 1916, some 1,200 separatists occupied buildings across Dublin, triggering a battle for what was then one of the major cities of the British Empire. Beyond the capital, poorly armed rebel contingents turned out in north Dublin, Meath, Louth, Galway and Wexford. Posters were a major tool for the broad dissemination of information during the rebellion and were distributed widely to garner support, urge action, boost morale and carry warnings. This public notice poster was issued by General John Maxwell (1859–1929) at the same time that he was presiding over the execution of the leaders of the 1916 Rising, as well as extensive martial laws and the internment of thousands of men and women in its aftermath. This poster aimed to prohibit GAA matches from taking place.

Although not formally involved in the 1916 Rising, the GAA made a significant contribution indirectly by producing a generation of physically fit young men with nationalist views and a hostility towards the government, state institutions and the forces of law and order. Members of the GAA were prominent in the Irish Volunteers and hurls commonly appeared in place of guns in drill and training exercises.

In the aftermath of the 1916 Rising, the Official Commission of Inquiry identified the GAA as an instigating factor in the rebellion. The GAA leadership denied this finding and later sought to engage with the British authorities to safeguard the organisation's sporting operations. This involved the GAA's exclusion from an entertainment tax and the reintroduction of special train services to matches.

PUBLIC NOTICE

POLITICAL MEETINGS, PARADES, OR PROCESSIONS

I, GENERAL SIR JOHN GRENFELL MAXWELL, K.C.B., K.C.M.G., C.V.O., D.S.O., Commanding-in-Chief His Majesty's Forces in Ireland, hereby Order that no Parade, Procession, or Political Meeting, or organized Football, Athletic, or Hurling Meeting, shall take place anywhere in Ireland without the written authority, previously obtained, of the Local County Inspector of Royal Irish Constabulary, or, in Dublin City, of the Chief Commissioner of the Dublin Metropolitan Police.

J. G. MAXWELL,
General, Commanding-in-Chief, The Forces in Ireland.

HEADQUARTERS, IRISH COMMAND,
11th May, 1916.

(281.) Wt. 557/G. 88.   5,000, 5, '16.   FALCONER, DUBLIN.

23. Rounders Bat (*c*.1922)

Kilmainham Gaol Museum (Loan)

During the Irish Civil War (1922–1923), hundreds of women were imprisoned in various holding centres around the country. Among them was Sighle Humphreys (1899–1994), a committed political activist who was deeply involved in the republican cause. She was imprisoned on several occasions for her part in campaigns organised by Cumann na mBan and the Irish Republican Army (IRA). In 1928, Sighle was imprisoned for smashing the windows of shopkeepers who flew union flags during the Tailteann Games.

While imprisoned, Sighle and other female internees highlighted their political status by engaging in hunger strikes, protests and tunnel digging. There were also many non-arduous aspects of prison life as the women led an ordered existence involving entertainment, games and sports. Diary entries by Cecilia Saunders Gallagher, when she was a political prisoner in Kilmainham Gaol in 1923, recall how Sighle regularly organised games of rounders in the exercise yard, as well as handball, Irish classes and various other activities.

This rounders bat was used by Sighle and is shaped from the leg of a wooden chair. It still retains a visual cue to its original purpose, but in its remodelled form as sports equipment, it embodies the complex relationship between prisoners and the things they make, use and recycle to survive prison life. Playing rounders and other sports contributed to the physical, mental and social wellness of prisoners and had a positive effect on prison communities. Rounders was a particularly popular sport in prison as it required basic equipment and could be played in areas with limited space, such as the exercise yard in Kilmainham Gaol.

24. Bootlace from Bloody Sunday (1920)

GAA Museum, Croke Park (on loan from Teresa Ryan, Tipperary)

On 21 November 1920, the Tipperary football team were travelling to the capital by train ahead of their challenge match against Dublin the following day. The match took a dreadful turn as Crown forces entered Croke Park and opened fire on the thousands of spectators. This marked a turning point in the Irish War of Independence on a day that would become known as Bloody Sunday.

Tipperary player Bill Ryan (1894–1991) boarded the train at Templemore. Later in the journey, a group of soldiers came on board at Ballybrophy and a brawl ensued involving some of the Tipperary players. Bill had his football boots thrown out of the train window. The following day, as the players were in the Croke Park dressing room preparing for the game, Bill bemoaned to his teammate Michael Hogan that his replacement boots were too loose. Hogan returned to his kitbag and pulled out a spare lace which he gave to Ryan to tighten around his boots before they took to the field.

Hogan was one of the fourteen civilians who lost their lives as shots were fired in the stadium a few minutes into the match. The incident followed the assassination earlier that day of twelve suspected British intelligence agents by Michael Collins's squad and was followed later that evening by the killing of two leading Dublin IRA officers and a civilian at Dublin Castle. It is thought that between 60 and 100 people suffered injuries from Bloody Sunday and many experienced trauma that cannot be measured. The bootlace, which was a seemingly unremarkable part of pre-match preparations between teammates, became a precious memento of the darkest day in the history of the GAA. Bill kept the bootlace for the rest of his life and was the last surviving player of the Bloody Sunday match.

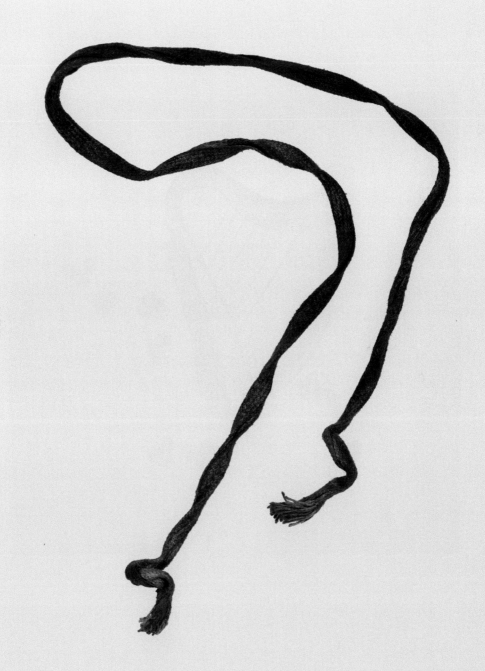

25. Sideline Flag from Ballykinlar Internment Camp (1921)

© National Museum of Ireland

Ballykinlar internment camp was the first mass prison camp established by the British authorities in Ireland during the War of Independence (1919–1921). Located in the shadows of the Mourne Mountains in Co. Down, the camp held up to 2,000 Irishmen who were suspected of republican activity. Camp conditions were harsh, but internees found the time and energy to play many sports, including Gaelic games. This sideline flag is made from a handkerchief, and was used during a football match in the camp in April 1921. The match was between two teams of prisoners, one of which was known as 'The Shamrocks' and the other 'The Harps', hence the hand-drawn decorations. The flag is painted in watercolour and ink by artist Joseph Bracken (1885–1930), who completed many illustrations of camp life during his internment.

Athletics in all its branches was essential to daily life in Ballykinlar. To prevent the stagnation and deterioration of the prisoners, it was necessary to keep them fit in both body and mind. The camp had a GAA board who organised various leagues and championship matches, and the space where they played out those competitions was given the name Croke Park.

Ballykinlar parish has a vibrant GAA community and history, and the local club facility was a training base for Down senior teams for a number of years. The site of the internment camp itself has a varied history, acting as a military base and training facility from the First World War until the 1980s. The site has been approved as the location for a state-of-the-art Centre of Excellence for Down GAA, securing Ballykinlar's status as an important site in the GAA's past, present and future.

26. Haughney Memorial Cup (1922)

Carlow County Museum and Cumann Lúthchleas Gael Coiste Chontae Ceatharlach

The Haughney Memorial Cup was first played for in 1922 in memory of Denis 'Buller' Haughney (1895–1922) who played football for Graiguecullen and Carlow. In the first round of the 1922 Carlow senior football championship, Haughney played in the forwards as Graiguecullen faced Palatine. As he and clubmate Willie Hogan jumped for a throw ball, they accidentally collided with each other and Haughney received a forceful knee to the stomach. Haughney was conveyed to the County Infirmary, where doctors declared that he was very badly hurt. He died of his injuries in hospital three days later, on 27 June 1922, with his death certificate stating that it was the result of accidental injuries to his abdomen. Haughney's coffin was draped with a tricolour, his IRA soldier's uniform and the football jersey he wore when playing that fateful match. He was buried in the republican plot in St Mary's cemetery in Carlow town.

The Haughney Memorial Cup was presented at a meeting of the Carlow county board four months after Haughney's death in the hope that it would be cherished by all of his colleagues. It was first played for in a special memorial tournament and was later presented to the winners of the Carlow senior football championship. Fittingly, Haughney's club, Graiguecullen, was the first team to have its name engraved on the cup when it won the title in 1925. Ballymurphy were the last winners of the cup in 1953, as a new one was introduced the following year.

G.A.A.

The Haughney Memorial Cup

Presented by Michael Governey Esq.
Chairman U.D.C. Carlow
· 1922 ·

Co. Carlow C'ships
· 1925 ·
Won by
Fraigue Cullen

· Won by ·
1926. Milford.
1927. O'hanrahans.
1928. O'hanrahans.
1929. Leighlinbridge.
1930. O'hanrahans.
1931. O'hanrahans.
1932. O'hanrahans.
1933. Milford.
1934. Tinryland.
1935. Kilbride.
1936. Tinryland.

65

27. Sam Maguire's Pocket Watch (1923)

GAA Museum, Croke Park

Sam Maguire (1877–1926) achieved posthumous fame when the All-Ireland senior football trophy was presented in his memory by his friends in 1928 after fundraising efforts. Before this, in 1923, his friends gave him another notable gift in the form of this gold pocket watch. At the time, a pocket watch like this with an elaborate design would have been considered a status symbol affordable only to the elite. Placed inside the pocket of a three-piece suit, it was a cultural marker and a means to perform punctuality. On the inside, this pocket watch is engraved: 'Presented to Sam Maguire by his fellow Gaels in London on his return to Ireland Jan 1923'.

A native of Dunmanway, Co. Cork, Maguire moved to London in the 1890s with his two brothers Dick and Jack, where they all immersed themselves in the London GAA scene. As well as this, Maguire was involved in the Gaelic League and the Irish Republican Brotherhood, which was a small, secret revolutionary body whose sole objective was to establish and maintain a free and independent republican government in Ireland. During the War of Independence, Maguire used his position working in the postal service in London to smuggle arms to Ireland and to intercept official state documents relevant to British military and political intentions at home.

In 1907, Maguire was elected chairman of the London county board and later a trustee of Croke Park, where he played in three All-Ireland football finals as captain of the London team. This pocket watch is a signifier of the esteem in which he was held by his peers in GAA circles in London.

28. Gold Medal from Tailteann Games (1924)

Melbourne Cricket Club

The first ancient Olympic Games took place in Greece 776 BC. By this time, the Tailteann Games, a thirty-day annual sports festival that was held in Co. Meath, was almost 100 years old, as it is said to have begun in 632 BC. The gathering included events such as foot racing and stone throwing, and it survived until the Norman invasion in AD 1169.

When the Games were revived by the GAA in Croke Park in 1924, they were intended to coincide with the Paris Olympics in order to attract international athletes. In all, twenty-four medal winners from the Paris Olympics competed in the Tailteann Games. One of the athletes was Ivan Stedman (1895–1979), an Australian swimmer who competed in freestyle and breast-stroke events at the Olympics. He won silver in Paris and two gold medals, one silver and one bronze at the Tailteann Games. Prior to being a competitive sportsman, Sted-man had served on the Western Front with the Australian Imperial Force in the First World War. His aquatic skills were used during the war when he rescued a British soldier who got into difficulty whilst swimming in the dark waters of the Hallue River. For this, Stedman received an award from the Royal Humane Society, London.

This gold medal features a crowned head of Queen Tailte, the patron deity of the Tailteann Games and foster mother of Ireland's first High King, Lugh of the Long Arm. The inscription reads 'An Bainrioghan Tailte' and the reverse features Celtic designs, the crests of the four provinces of Ireland and an inscription that reads 'SWIMMING'. The Tailteann Games were held again in 1928 and 1932 but peaked in 1924 by bringing positive international atten-tion and much-needed tourism in the aftermath of the Irish Civil War.

29. Diary of US Tour (1926)

Lár na Páirce, Thurles

In May 1926, twenty-three people set sail for America on a tour that was intended as a fundraiser and to promote Gaelic Games overseas. These representatives of the 1925 Tipperary All-Ireland-winning hurling team played a series of matches against GAA teams in New York, Boston, Chicago and San Francisco. This is a handwritten diary kept by one of the players, Thomas J. Kenny from Portroe, during his time on the tour. It begins on 10 May 1926 before the group set sail from Cobh to New York on the SS *Bremen* – a German ocean liner. The diary goes on to record impressions, incidents and experiences from the eleven-week tour and was published in book form in 1928.

The voyage took almost ten days and on arriving in New York, the team, in full hurling gear, marched from the boat to motor cars that conveyed them to City Hall where they were greeted by the Mayor of New York, J.J. Walker. This tour of the US was by all means a triumph in comparison to the 1888 American Invasion Tour, which resulted in financial difficulties for the GAA, the abandonment of the All-Ireland final (which was due to be played in New York) and many of the touring party staying in the US never again to return to Ireland. Thomas's hopes for 'a successful, never to be forgotten tour', which he writes about in the first page of the diary, were realised as the team were 'received by a spirit of friendship everywhere'. The last page of the diary includes the signatures of all the players on the tour.

30. Account Book from Gaelic Field, Dungarvan (c.1927)

Waterford County Museum

The Gaelic Field at Shandon, Dungarvan is the original home ground of Waterford GAA. It was initially used for Gaelic games, athletics, agricultural shows and even for visiting circuses. This account book, kept by Dan Fraher (1852–1929), shows the meticulous details of attendances, stewards on duty and gate receipts. He was an athlete, Irish language promoter and GAA administrator, who drove the development of the field and personally purchased the land in 1912. Fraher also played a major role in the purchase of the Jones' Road site (Croke Park) for the GAA's national stadium. Many important games have been contested in Dungarvan, including the All-Ireland hurling finals of 1905 and 1907.

This page of the account book lists the names of individuals who were involved in match-day operations and collecting entry fees at the gates in pounds, shillings and pence. There were three viewing points to watch the game from: the field, stand or sideline. Not only

does the account book give insight into how business was conducted and recorded but also into the championship schedule, which was played in the autumn, with the Munster final played five weeks after the semi-final. There were 2,000 more supporters recorded at the semi-final (Tipperary versus Cork) than the final (Tipperary versus Limerick). Limerick played that Munster final just three weeks after losing the 1923 All-Ireland final to Galway, which was delayed due to the tumultuous revolutionary years.

The account book indicates that the financial management of matches and utilising Gaelic games as a business venture is not just a modern phenomenon, but a necessary practice in fortifying and promoting the sport, as well as maintaining the Gaelic Field as a viable location for championship encounters. Major improvements to the venue were carried out in the 1990s and it now bears the name Fraher Field in Dan's honour.

Total Gate & Total number of people who attend the
Feed. Cork v Tipperary Semi # Senior Hurling 1924

1924
August 31 .

		@			
662 S	4-	331	5	6
1518	4-	151	15	S
375	4/-	75	1	3
8518	.S	558	2	4

2/- Transfer Gate does not Count

8 15 9
£566 / 18 / 1

1924
October 5 Limerick v Tipperary Final Senior
Hurling Munster Championships

numbers of Persons. Field	4765	239	4	9
Stand	1438	151	16	6
Side Line	383	105	12	6
	6586	£496	13	9

the Field was £92 Less than
aug st 31st above
Stand about equal
Side Line was £21 15 . 4 more

4/- Gate 1 Wm O Donnell	30	3	9
2 John. O Donnell	15	10	
3 Pk Maher	23	7	
4 Pk O Donnell	20	12	6
5 Tom Dalton	17	14	3
6 Pk Condon	20	18	2
7 Pk Ormonde	26	17	6
8 Tom Fahey	24	8	6
9 Tom Walsh	25		
10 P. McGrath	16	14	
11 E. O Donohoe	8	13	
12 A. Mason	8	5	3
13 Motor Cars			

Total Field £239 4 9

Stand 2/- Jenny Riely	58 15 0				
2 Bob Luttey	35 -2 0	.			
3 George Lennon	20				
4 Wm Fitzgerald	21. 8 6				
5 P. Whelan	5/8				
6 Conny McGrath	1. 11.				
7 E. Power	14	£143	8	6

Side Line 4/- Joe Wyse	48.12 0			
Byrne	29. 2	76	14	
H. Par Reg transfer from Field		8	8	
Transfer from Field to Side Line J Casey		9	17	
Transfer from Stand to Side Line Wm Meehan	19 1 6			

£496 13.

31. *The Tipperary Hurler* by Seán Keating (1928)

The Hugh Lane Gallery

The Tipperary Hurler is one of the only significant GAA-themed paintings in state ownership and was painted in 1928 by Seán Keating (1889–1977). For more than seventy years, Keating worked as an artist, an art teacher and a broadcaster. He became one of the principal painters of the Irish Free State and had a deep interest in painting emerging history. He often transformed ordinary men into idealised and heroic figures, just like the hurler in this artwork.

Keating began this painting in 1925, based on a sketch he made at the All-Ireland final of John-Joe Hayes, who played at half-back for Tipperary when they won the final comfortably against Galway. The Tipperary team were described as 'bewildering in their brilliance'. After becoming distracted by another commission, Keating did not finish *The Tipperary Hurler* immediately and put the incomplete canvas aside. Three years later, Keating finished the painting using a different model, Ben O'Hickey from Bansha, Co. Tipperary, a student at the Dublin Metropolitan School of Art who 'looked extraordinarily like Hayes'. Despite the title of the painting, the red jersey and green sash bearing the initials 'C.H.C.' do not belong to a Tipperary team but a Dublin club – Commercials Hurling Club. The club was established in the Phoenix Park in 1886 and relocated to Rathcoole in 1979 after securing its own grounds. Their jerseys still bear the same vibrant colours as depicted by Keating.

The painting was first exhibited in Amsterdam as part of the Olympic Games in 1928, when art was still an Olympic discipline. It was taken out of storage in 2009 and hung in the Hugh Lane Gallery amid anticipated strong public interest ahead of Tipperary's appearance in the All-Ireland hurling final.

32. John Joe Doyle's Protective Goggles (1930s)

Clare Museum, Ennis

John Joe 'Goggles' Doyle (1906–2000) was a Clare hurler from Newmarket-on-Fergus, who played at left corner-back for the Clare senior hurling team from 1926 to 1938. He wore glasses and in order to protect them while playing hurling, he made his own protective goggles.

Hurling almost lost John Joe entirely in his very early days, as he thought about quitting the game when he found he could not play unless he wore his glasses. With contact lenses not becoming widespread until after John Joe's hurling career was over, his glasses lenses were broken on numerous occasions, causing cuts to his eyebrow necessitating stitches. John Joe wrote to England and the US to source a pair of suitable guards for his glasses, but found those worn by baseball players, motor cyclists and stone breakers would not suit his purposes on the hurling field. So he conceived the idea of making his own protective covering for his glasses when he failed to procure anything from other avenues. He designed and made these using rust-proof bicycle spokes, medical bandages and elastic. John Joe's homemade goggles apparently in no way affected his game and earned him the affectionate nickname by which he was known.

John Joe won six Clare senior hurling championship medals with his club, Newmarket-on-Fergus, winning his first in 1925. He captained Clare in the 1932 All-Ireland final versus Kilkenny, which they lost 2–3 to 3–3. This would be the county's last appearance in the All-Ireland hurling final until 1995. When Clare beat Galway in the semi-final that year, John Joe celebrated in the dressing rooms with the players afterwards and promised to bring his famous goggles to the All-Ireland final once again.

33. Henry Kenny's Leather Boots (*c.*1930s)

Private Collection (Henry Kenny Junior, Ballyvary)

These boots of thick leather were worn by Henry Kenny (1913–1975), a footballer from Castlebar who won many accolades at club and provincial level, as well as a coveted first All-Ireland championship title with the Mayo team of 1936. The team did not discuss their achievements at length and this hesitancy to brandish their win was reflected in Sam Maguire's first appearance in the county, which was a reserved one. Instead of a joyous homecoming greeted by thousands of elated supporters, captain of the team Seamus O'Malley (1903–2002) returned to Claremorris with the trophy in the back of a hired car as he reported for his teaching duties in the local national school the morning after the final.

This type of heavy boot was laced up to the ankle to protect the player's feet but gave limited flexibility. A continuous improvement in shoe design and synthetic materials means that modern boots are considerably lighter, with particular stability features and even the ability to influence kicking accuracy. However, Henry shrugged off these advances and described modern boots as 'slippers'. He usually bought his boots in a small size but gave them to a friend, Boston Bennett, who would 'break in' the boots for him. Bennett would put dubbing that was used for horse saddles on the boots and wear them for a couple of training sessions to soften the leather and to stretch them before returning them to Henry.

When Henry traded football for politics and was elected a TD for Mayo South and Mayo West in 1954, it marked the beginning of a succession of the Kenny family in politics. His sons have been involved at local and national level, with Henry Junior serving as Fine Gael councillor in Mayo for twenty-four years and Enda becoming Taoiseach in 2011.

34. Hurleymaker's Spokeshave (c.1930s)

Torpey Hurleys, Sixmilebridge

The original hurleys may have been nothing more than a shepherd's crook, but today's hurleys are the product of generations of experience and experimentation. This spokeshave is a hand tool used in woodworking to shave curved pieces of wood down to the required size. It was used by Patrick 'Pop' Torpey when he began to make hurleys in the 1930s for local players in Sixmilebridge and Kilkishen in East Clare. The key feature of this spokeshave is the low angle of the blade so that it is suited to the task of hurley making. The tool could be used for both fine work in refining the shape of hurleys and also for the rapid removal of wood. Crafting hurleys by hand was a slow process which has since been replaced with machinery.

The tradition of hurley making involves passing on the knowledge and skills required to craft what is the most important equipment for hurlers. The Torpey family is now in its third generation of hurley makers and has been at the forefront of innovation of design and production. Patrick's nephew John, who won a junior All-Ireland hurling title with Wicklow in 1967, formally established Torpey Hurleys as a business in 1981. John introduced the modern hurley grip as a staple of hurling equipment and paved the path for his son Seán to develop the business further and participate in pioneering research and design.

The dwindling quantities of ash trees in Ireland has been a concern for hurley makers for many years. Since 2012, ash dieback disease (a highly destructive fungal infection) has been spreading across ash plantations in Ireland, forcing makers to come up with alternatives to ash hurls. Torpeys have developed a hurley made from bamboo, one of the fastest-growing, renewable resources in the world, and in doing so, are building on past techniques to evolve the craft of hurley making.

35. Fermanagh Exiles Team Sash (1930)

Fermanagh County Museum Collection, Museum Services,
Fermanagh & Omagh District Council

This is the sash of the Fermanagh Exiles team who won the New York junior football championship in 1930. The final was played at Innisfail Park in the Bronx, which later changed its name to Gaelic Park and became the home of Gaelic games in New York. Throughout the 1920s and 1930s, the tide of Irish immigrants to New York meant that GAA clubs flourished.

At a meeting of Fermanagh Gaelic Football Club held in April 1930, it was decided that the Fermanagh Exiles colours would be white with a green sash and the word 'Fermanagh' in gold letters. The gold letters did not transpire, but the sash was kept with the traditional Fermanagh colours of green and white. In reporting the decision, the *Fermanagh Herald* newspaper wrote: 'Even divided as we are by the broad Atlantic, our colours are still the same.' The long strip of fabric was worn uniformly over the right shoulder. In formal military attire, sashes denote rank and authority, so the captain and vice-captain had sashes of the same style and colour distinguishing their roles in writing.

The Fermanagh Exiles club has been formed and reformed on many occasions under different names, the first being in 1930. When the Fermanagh Gaelic Football Club of New York was established in 1963, it was having difficulty recruiting a full team, and put a notice in the newspaper at home that anyone interested in football and contemplating emigration to the US should contact the president of the new club. Since 1948, the cup presented to the winners of the Fermanagh senior club championship has been courtesy of Fermanagh immigrants in New York. The O'Dwyer Cup was bought by the Fermanaghmen's Association in New York for $164 and was in use for fifty years. In 1998, it was retired and replaced with a new cup purchased from funds raised by the Fermanagh GAA club in New York.

36. South Africa Flag from Tailteann Games (1932)

Lár na Páirce, Thurles

When the Tailteann Games took place in 1932, it was not only a sporting competition but an opportunity for athletes to travel from overseas. Many countries were represented in events such as high jump and swimming, but there were fewer who took part in the Gaelic games competitions. A hurling team from South Africa competed and flew this flag at the official opening ceremony in Croke Park. Seven members of the hurling team were born in South Africa to Irish parents, demonstrating the importance of the diaspora in disseminating the tradition of GAA overseas.

South Africa's participation in the Tailteann Games was initiated when a public representative of the Union of South Africa, E.K. Scallan, visited Ireland in 1923 and boasted of the country's abundance of promising runners and handballers. Athletes from South Africa participated in the first Tailteann Games the following year, in lawn tennis and boxing among other events. For South Africa's appearance at the Tailteann Games in 1932, a community of Irish nuns in Capetown designed this flag and presented it to the travelling party. Embroidered with South Africa in both Irish and English, the design merges the layout of the South African flag at the time and the colours of the Irish tricolour.

Gaelic games have proved successful with South Africans as they have no political legacy in the country and have the potential to fulfil a vital role in the country's social development. In 2016, a GAA team travelled to Ireland to represent South Africa and compete in the GAA World Games. The South African Gaels team was comprised of indigenous players and perhaps a trick was missed that this flag was not reused as delegates represented the country under the auspices of the GAA once again.

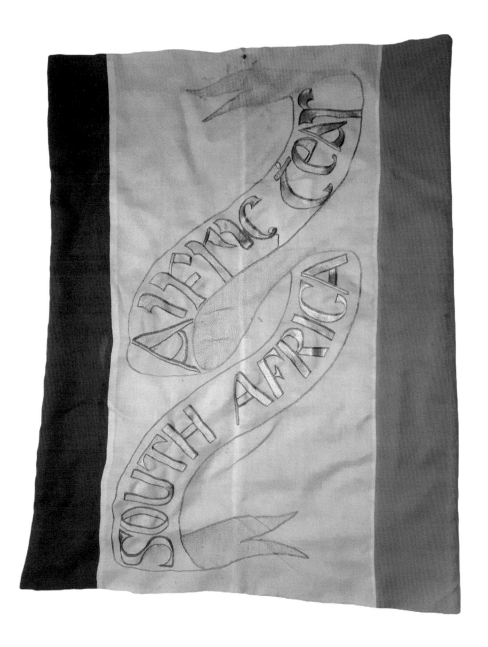

37. Gold Pin from Camogie Tournament (1933)

Kilmurry Independence Museum

This gold cross pin was presented to each member of the Muskerry team who won the Courtmacsherry camogie tournament in October 1933. Also known as the Muskerry Maids, they beat Fermoy by three goals to two in a replay after the first game ended in a draw a month earlier. Rev. John Sheedy (1890–1938), who organised the tournament, put up a set of gold pins and a silver cup for the winners, as well as a set of silver medals for the runners-up. His aim was to develop and encourage sport among girls and help the development of Courtmacsherry – a seaside village in west Cork. Crafted in 9ct gold, the Celtic cross is richly carved on the front, with the back displaying the engraving 'Courtmacsherry Camogie T'ment 1933'.

Muskerry enjoyed great camogie success in 1933 when they won the Cork county championship and the Clonakilty Cup, beating Macroom on St Stephen's Day. Kate Delea, who played in the forwards for the Muskerry Maids, went on to captain the Cork camogie team to their first All-Ireland title in 1934 – the first camogie final to be played in Croke Park. This began a hat-trick of titles for Cork from 1934 to 1936. The 1930s was a prosperous era for camogie in Cork, with almost every secondary school in the county having a camogie team, but it was also tainted by a split in the county over the GAA imposing a ban on foreign games, which were viewed as detrimental to the national games. In 1934, the Camogie Association adopted a six-month suspension on camogie players found to be playing the game of hockey. This approach inevitably damaged camogie and some Cork camogie teams left the board over the matter. Nevertheless, Cork persevered and again captured three titles in a row from 1939 to 1941, with many Muskerry players on the team.

38. GAA Golden Jubilee Postage Stamp (1934)

An Post

Commemorative postage stamps have been issued annually since 1929 and featured subjects such as the centenary of Catholic Emancipation (1929), the Shannon Scheme (1930), the 200th anniversary of the Royal Dublin Society (1931) and the Eucharistic Congress (1932). An Post issued a special twopenny stamp to commemorate the golden jubilee of the GAA in 1934, which went on sale from July until the end of the year. Other commemorative events for the 50th anniversary of the GAA included an 'Irish Ireland' concert in the Gaiety Theatre, an essay competition for schoolchildren, and a pipe band contest which took place during the opening procession parade of the golden jubilee celebrations on 9 September 1934.

A public notice was published in national newspapers inviting designers to submit their GAA stamp designs, with the winner selected by a committee of distinguished artists. The winning design was by Richard King, who also designed the Holy Year stamp of a similar style for An Post in 1932. King was an astute glass designer who created the Kevin Barry Memorial window at University College Dublin. The stamp features a figure of a hurler with camán in action surmounted by the word 'Eire'. Under the dates 1884 and 1934 are Cúmann Lúith-Chleas Gaedheal, all in Gaelic characters.

The stamp received a mixed reception at the time. In February 1935, the Hillside football club in Cork requested that the government adopt the special stamp as the permanent twopenny stamp of the Irish Free State. On the other side, remarks were made about how the stamp perpetuated the sameness and monotony of Irish stamp design. The *Kerry Reporter* newspaper commented on the disappointment of hurling being chosen to represent the GAA on the commemorative stamp. The argument was that Gaelic football should also have been represented, but such is the challenge of effectively conveying a message via the smallest of media.

WILL'S CIGARETTES.

D. WALSH,
(OFFALY).

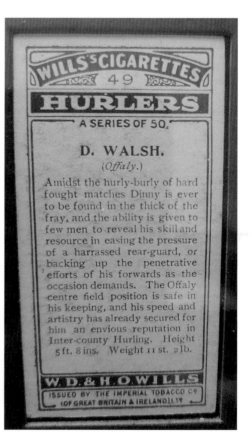

WILL's CIGARETTES

49

HURLERS

A SERIES OF 50.

D. WALSH.
(Offaly.)

Amidst the hurly-burly of hard
fought matches Dinny is ever
to be found in the thick of the
fray, and the ability is given to
few men to reveal his skill and
resource in easing the pressure
of a harrassed rear-guard, or
backing up the penetrative
efforts of his forwards as the
occasion demands. The Offaly
centre field position is safe in
his keeping, and his speed and
artistry has already secured for
him an envious reputation in
Inter-county Hurling. Height
5 ft. 8 ins. Weight 11 st. 2 lb.

W.D. & H.O. WILLS

ISSUED BY THE IMPERIAL TOBACCO Cº
(OF GREAT BRITAIN & IRELAND) Lᵗᵈ

39. Collectable Cigarette Card (c.1930s)

Private Collection (Jim Whelan, Graiguenamanagh)

Between 1900 and 1940, cartophily, as the hobby was known, became widespread as hundreds of millions of attractive cards were issued globally, usually with packets of cigarettes. The cards featured a wide array of topics, from military and sport history to nature and geography. Will's cigarettes issued a series of cards that featured hurlers and footballers, with a portrait on the front and a short biography on the back. This card is one from a series of fifty cards which includes hurlers from Clare, Cork, Dublin, Galway, Kilkenny, Leix (Laois), Limerick, Offaly and Tipperary. It features Dinny Walsh, who was a dual player with Tullamore and Offaly in the 1920s before he emigrated to the US and played on the Offaly team that won several New York championships. It was hoped that featuring GAA players on the cards would build brand loyalty as smokers collected the entire series. An additional purpose of the cards was to prevent the cigarettes from getting damaged. During the First World War, relatives of prisoners of war were instructed to remove the collector's cards from cigarettes when sending them in parcels for fear that any pictures of an 'offensive nature towards Germany' would result in the cigarette packets being confiscated. The cards were collected by young and old alike, with schoolchildren often waiting outside shops to ask adult customers for their tobacco cards. Albums were issued in which each card could be pasted and carefully stored. The heyday of tobacco card manufacturers ended in the 1940s as chewing gum manufacturers entered the market. In 1963, Dublin-based confectionery company Liam Devlin & Sons created a series cards with recognisable GAA personalities, including hurlers, footballers, camogie players, handballers and one referee, John Dowling.

40. Mullingar Town Trophy (1934)

Mullingar Shamrocks GAA Club

The Mullingar Town trophy is distinctly original in its form as a GAA trophy and was first played for in 1935 in a competition featuring the top four teams in the country at the time: Mayo, Dublin, Kildare and Tipperary. It was commissioned by the traders of Mullingar the year before to commemorate the GAA's golden jubilee and presented to Westmeath GAA. In making the presentation, the Mullingar Traders 'did so on behalf of the people of Mullingar as a token of esteem and to co-operate in the good work the GAA were doing'.

The trophy was designed and created by Percy Oswald Reeves (1870–1967), a teacher at the Dublin Metropolitan School of Art and a highly skilled craftsman. Conceived as a symbolic 'tower of strength', it is a rectangular, figural, four-sided trophy in copper and enamelled in warm scarlet, turquoise, yellow, black and white. One of the panels shows hurls and footballs; another depicts a hooded, athletic and naked male representing Cú Chulainn, heroically poised with a handball above two charging horses' heads which are set with gold and silver bridles. A third panel has an engraved inscription stating the occasion and origin of the trophy. The trophy is set on a pedestal of Kilkenny marble and around the base are the arms of the four provinces.

Upon presenting the trophy, the stipulations were that the trophy could not be won outright and all matches must be played in Cusack Park, Mullingar. It was later decided that it would be an intercounty trophy which would help clear off the debt from Cusack Park and bring prosperity to the town. It eventually became a tournament between Westmeath clubs and was played on an irregular basis, with the trophy last played for in 1992.

41. Waterford GAA Calendar Poster (1937)

Waterford County Museum

By the 1920s, calendar posters had become a popular means of advertising and were mass-produced quickly and cheaply. Waterford GAA capitalised on this trend by creating a poster advertising various prominent businesses in Waterford city and county. The calendar is secondary to the advertising as it is notably small and difficult to read. The poster lists the county champions and the officials and members of the Waterford county board for 1937. It represents a nexus between modern commercial imagery, a celebration of the Waterford county champions and recognition of its committee for the year to follow. A poster of almost identical design was commissioned by Fermanagh GAA in 1935 and by Cavan GAA in 1940. All of these posters were printed and published in Dublin by Irish Annuals Press Ltd, whose elaborate corner building at 16/17 Lower O'Connell Street was built as part of the reconstruction of the street after the 1916 Rising.

The central image on the poster is of the De La Salle college team who won the Waterford senior football title in 1936. De La Salle was a teacher training institution from 1881 before being converted into a secondary school in 1923. Today, De La Salle GAA club maintains connections with the De La Salle Brothers and continues to have a strong GAA legacy. The 1936 team featured Seamus Ó Riain (1916–2007) from Moneygall, Co. Tipperary, who attended teacher training at the college. He would go on to become president of the GAA from 1967 to 1970 and oversaw many visionary initiatives during his tenure including Féile na nGael, Scór, Australian Rules games, the development of GAA clubs as social centres within the community and the decision to build a modern handball court in Croke Park.

42. Scissors used to open the Cusack Stand (1938)

GAA Museum, Croke Park

When the Cusack Stand in Croke Park was opened in 1938, it marked a milestone in the GAA progressing as an organisation and meeting the growing demands of the games and its spectators. The two-tier stand comprised 6,000 seats and room for 16,000 standing underneath and was the largest of its kind in Europe at the time. The opening of the stand was a highly anticipated event and GAA President Pádraig MacNamee (1896–1975) used these scissors to perform the official opening, which took place at half-time during the All-Ireland senior football semi-final between Kerry and Laois.

The naming of the stand after GAA founder Michael Cusack resulted from a motion at the Central Council from Sean McCarthy (Munster Council chairman), who also suggested that, if possible, a team from each of the four provinces should play on the occasion of the opening of the stand. This suggestion was accomplished as the junior hurlers of Galway and Antrim played in the first match of the afternoon, Dublin played Antrim in the minor hurling semi-final and Kerry took on Laois in the All-Ireland senior football semi-final.

The stand itself, made of reinforced concrete, cost £50,000 and was erected by Limerick-based contractors Messrs McCaffrey and O'Carroll. On the opening day, a place of honour was reserved in the stand for winners of All-Ireland championship medals, as well as past presidents and members of the provincial and Central councils. The price for a seat in the Cusack Stand on its opening day was two shillings and could be purchased from one of the twenty-eight turnstiles at the St James's Avenue end. The stand has since been renovated and replaced, but the same tradition has endured since 1938 as thousands of spectators take their seats in the stand that bears Cusack's name.

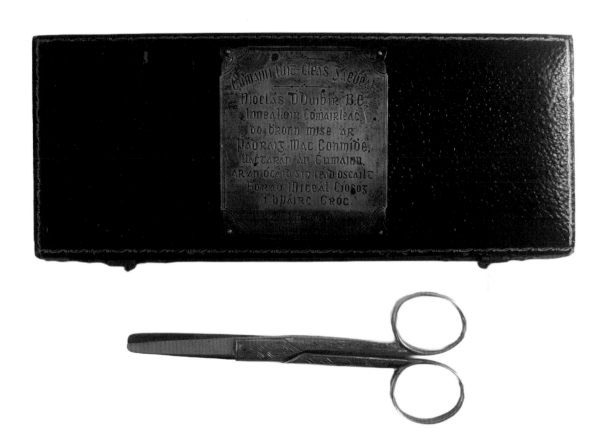

43. 'Thunder and Lightning' Final Ticket (1939)

GAA Museum, Croke Park

On 3 September 1939, in response to Adolf Hitler's invasion of Poland, Britain and France declared war on Germany. The news was broken by Prime Minister Neville Chamberlain (1869–1940) at 11.15 a.m. in a five-minute broadcast on the BBC. In Croke Park, the outbreak of international conflict seemed a million miles away as Kilkenny took on Cork in the All-Ireland hurling final in front of a crowd of almost 40,000 supporters. This is a ticket to that match, which admitted the holder to the Cusack Stand at a cost of five shillings.

The match was played against a backdrop of violent thunderstorms and became known as the 'thunder and lightning' final. Practically all of the second half was fought in a thunderstorm accompanied by vivid flashes of lightning and a deluge of rain. Both teams appealed for the match to be called off owing to the weather conditions but the referee persevered. The tempo of the game was in keeping with the elements as it was a thriller with a dramatic last minute point securing victory for Kilkenny. James Phelan (1917–2006), who scored 2–1 for Kilkenny that day, described how it 'rained so hard that the black and amber colours of my jersey ran into my togs'.

Both sets of teams were aware of the news of the outbreak of the Second World War (1939–1945) before they took to the field, but their concentration was firmly on the hurling final. Dr Jim Young (1915–1992) was one of the Cork hurlers who learned of the outbreak of the war after attending Mass in Dublin that morning and later explained how 'we were so taken up trying to win the All-Ireland that we didn't realise the gravity of the situation'. That day, the All-Ireland hurling final was played in weather that reflected the peril of the political moment and the match is synonymous with the beginning of a period in Ireland known as 'The Emergency'.

44. Football from All-Ireland Final (1943)

Private Collection (Murray's Bar, Knockcroghery)

In 1943, the Roscommon footballers appeared in the All-Ireland senior football final for the first time. This was a particularly remarkable feat given that they had been a junior team just three years earlier. Roscommon beat Cavan to claim their first ever All-Ireland senior title and retained it again in 1944 by overcoming Kerry in the final.

Captain on both occasions was Jimmy Murray (1917–2007) from Knockcroghery, who played alongside his brother Phelim and three fellow club players – Liam Gilmartin, Jim Brennan and Johnny Briens. Jimmy ran the family businesses of a shop, pub, hardware store and undertakers in his native village. He claimed the leather football used in the 1943 final and proudly displayed it in the front window of Murray's Bar alongside his medals, jerseys and the coveted Sam Maguire trophy. Later, the football would hang from a string from the ceiling of the bar.

In 1990, a fire broke out on the premises, destroying half the bar counter and much of the main lounge. As the blaze was being fought by the fire brigade, one of the firemen shouted in triumph, 'I've got the ball! I've got the ball!' Jimmy's reply was 'Never mind the ball, put out the bloody fire!' And so, the ball survived – but not without damage, as the signatures of the Roscommon players were burnt off. Jimmy set about diligently rewriting the signatures of his teammates using a permanent black marker. This football is a reminder of how objects can survive and endure to allow us to retell our own stories, but that their wear and tear is a story in itself. The football continues to hang proudly from the ceiling over the bar in the family pub where Jimmy spent endless hours serving his locals and reminiscing about his days playing Gaelic football.

cumann lút-cleas ꜱaeꝺeal

ALL-IRELAND FOOTBALL

SEMI-   FINAL

KERRY *versus*
CARLOW

AT

CROKE PARK

ON

Sunday, 27th August, 1944

PROGRAMMES 2d. EACH

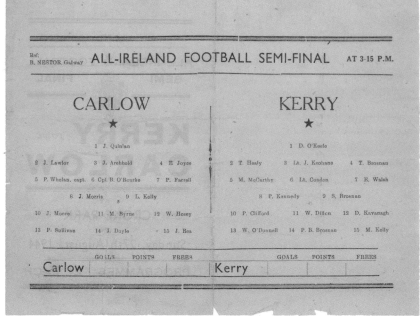

Ref:
B. NESTOR, Galway **ALL-IRELAND FOOTBALL SEMI-FINAL**   AT 3-15 P.M.

CARLOW
★

1 J. Quinlan		
2 J. Lawlor	3 J. Archbold	4 E. Joyce
5 P. Whelan, capt.	6 Cpl. B. O'Rourke	7 P. Farrell
8 J. Morris	9 L. Kelly	
10 J. Moore	11 M. Byrne	12 W. Hosey
13 P. Sullivan	14 J. Doyle	15 J. Rea

KERRY
★

1 D. O'Keefe		
2 T. Healy	3 Lt. J. Keohane	4 T. Brosnan
5 M. McCarthy	6 Lt. Condon	7 E. Walsh
8 P. Kennedy	9 S. Brosnan	
10 P. Clifford	11 W. Dillon	12 D. Kavanagh
13 W. O'Donnell	14 P. B. Brosnan	15 M. Kelly

	GOALS	POINTS	FREES		GOALS	POINTS	FREES
Carlow				Kerry			

45. Unofficial Match Programme (1944)

Carlow County Museum

Carlow football's first and only senior championship trophy came in 1944 when they won the Leinster title, beating Dublin and qualifying for an All-Ireland semi-final versus Kerry. The attendance of 40,727 set a new record for a semi-final, with £2,515 taken in gate receipts. Kerry won on a scoreline of 3–3 to 0–10 and in the days following the match, the Carlow county secretary sent a letter to the Kerry cohort congratulating them on their victory. Commenting on the letter, *The Kerryman* remarked how the letter made 'refreshing reading when one remembers the squeals raised and alibis made so often by beaten teams and their followers'. Carlow played Kerry again in October 1944 as part of a fundraiser for Austin Stack Memorial Park in Tralee.

Until 1975, the Leinster championship match-day programmes consisted of just one page folded over. This lent itself to the production of pirate editions of match programmes which were sold further away from GAA grounds. This meant that by the time supporters reached the grounds where the official programmes were being sold, they did not purchase them. This unofficial match programme was produced during a time when they were at their most popular, in the 1940s and 1950s. It was legal to sell these pirate publications provided that they were not described as official. However, these were often poorly printed, with basic information and limited reading content.

Match programmes are one of the most plentiful souvenirs of GAA matches but very few survive from this semi-final, which may be due to the adverse weather conditions. The torrential rain on the day of the Kerry versus Carlow match meant that many of those who were travelling by bike had to take shelter in farm buildings on the journey home from Croke Park.

46. Handball Medal found in South Africa (1946)

Private Collection (Joe Masterson, Rhode)

Rev. Fr Edward Kelly (1924–2013), a native of Tullow, Co. Carlow, was a missionary priest in South Africa and later curate in Rhode, Co. Offaly. He was stationed in Soweto from 1955 to 1972 and from 1974 to 1980. It was during one of these periods that Fr Kelly discovered this medal in a collection box in the church where he said Mass. The medal reads '1946 Bronnad ag Ard-Comhairle na h-Éireann C.L.L. [Cumann Liathróid Láimhe]' which translates as '1946 Central Council Presentation Irish Handball Association'. It is unknown who placed the medal in the collection box, or even if it was an intentional gesture, but Fr Kelly took it back to Ireland where he later placed it in the ownership of Joe Masterson, who served as president of GAA Handball from 2017 to 2020.

The medal dates to 1946, a time when the game of handball was popular in South Africa, especially among boys attending the Christian Brothers Schools at Boksburg, a suburb of Johannesburg. Handball was first introduced to South Africa in the early 1930s by the Irish diaspora and Irish priests based there. A key figure in the development of handball in South Africa was Brendan Muldoon, who was born in South Africa but sent back to Ireland to be educated at Knockbeg College in Co. Carlow. Muldoon appealed to county boards across Ireland to donate money towards South African handball funds and many obliged, including the Galway county board who donated £5. Fundraising allowed for the construction of handball alleys in South Africa and at one stage, there were seven handball clubs across the country.

While mystery still surrounds the medal, its original owner and how or why it ended up in Fr Kelly's collection box in Soweto, the medal has been given a new meaning as it has changed hands, travelled thousands of miles and been transformed from a personal possession to a shared souvenir.

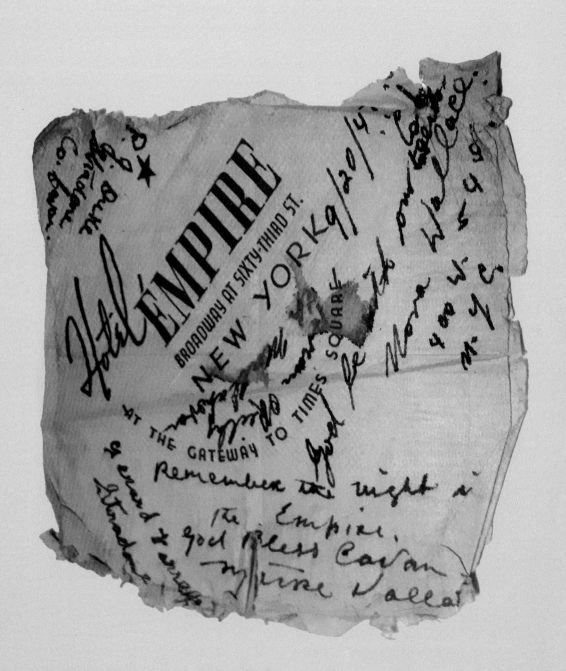

47. Napkin from Hotel Empire, New York (1947)

Cavan County Museum

In 1947, for the first and only time, the All-Ireland final was played outside of Ireland and contested by the footballers of Cavan and Kerry. The GAA took the final overseas as a gesture of goodwill towards the Irish community in the US, many of whom emigrated because of the Great Famine 100 years earlier. It was also hoped that the match would help promote Gaelic games in North America. The final in the Polo Grounds drew a crowd of 34,941 to see Cavan emerge victorious. Pádraig Ó Caoimh (1897–1964), general secretary of the GAA, declared the final a triumph as it 'enlightened the American public as to the separate existence and identity of the Irish people'.

This napkin was kept as a memento of the trip to New York by P.J. Duke (1925–1950), who played at half-back for Cavan. It is from the Hotel Empire, where the Cavan team stayed for the duration of their time in the city. The team were feted everywhere and there were many supporters calling to the hotel, which made it difficult for the players to get some peace and quiet. The napkin is signed by many individuals including P.J himself, some giving their addresses in Cavan and New York. The napkin was perhaps used as an impromptu address book to keep in touch with new friends made during the trip. The date written on the napkin is 20 September 1947, almost one week after the final and two days before the teams departed for home. The handwritten notes on the napkin such as 'God bless Cavan' and 'Remember that night in the Empire' are a mixture of the celebration of the occasion and anticipation of the nostalgia of their famous trip to the USA. Sadly, P.J.'s memories of that trip to New York would be short-lived as he died three years later from tuberculosis at the age of twenty-five.

48. Player's Please Figure (c.1940s)

Private Collection (James A. Lundon, Galway)

As an item of widespread everyday consumption in the 20th century, tobacco was enjoyed at all levels of society, which made it an important element in the economy and an essential source of state revenue. Similarly, the GAA's relationship with the tobacco trade centred on the need to protect the revenue it raised from advertising. This hand-painted figure made of plaster was used to advertise John Player's No.6 cigarettes at points of sales in shops and pubs. There are several versions of this statue with footballers and hurlers in different team colours. Reproductions have appeared but these original figures from the 1940s are now collector's items.

Player's No.6 was a particular brand of cigarette which sponsored a number of sports competitions in the 1970s including darts and angling in Co. Sligo, pitch and putt in Co. Cork and cricket and ladies' golf in Co. Dublin. Player's Please tobacco advertisements were common in match programmes and newspapers, one of many of the GAA's alliance with tobacco companies; P.J. Carroll sponsored the All-Star awards and overseas trips until 1978. When Limerick's Mick Mackey was inducted into the Texaco Hall of Fame in 1961, his prize was a silver cigarette case.

At the GAA Congress in 1977, a motion to abolish advertising of alcohol and tobacco at GAA grounds was heavily defeated, indicating the reliance upon income from such sponsorships. The GAA has since reappraised its attitude to sponsorship and cut all ties with tobacco companies in favour of encouraging the creation of tobacco-free GAA grounds to positively impact upon smoking behaviour.

49. Cap signed by Christy Ring (1952)

Cork Public Museum

This cap in the red and white of Cork was hand-made by Bill O'Regan from Mayfield. He was one of the 64,332 supporters in attendance at the All-Ireland hurling final in 1952, when Cork defeated Dublin 2–14 to 0–7. Commentary from the match remarked on how bright sunshine shone on Croke Park that September day, so Bill's cap was as practical as it was decorative.

Trains were an important service for travelling to matches when cars were scarce, and teams regularly took the train along with supporters, both often congregating in celebration. During the journey back to Cork after the team's victory, Bill got the peak of his cap signed by Christy Ring (1920–1979), who had won his sixth All-Ireland medal that day when he played at left half-forward. Ring dominated hurling in the 1950s and is widely regarded by players, commentators and supporters as one of the greatest hurlers in the history of the game. Ring's marker that day was Des 'Snitchy' Ferguson, who 'stayed with him like a shadow'.

Ring's signature on the cap, as with many autographed possessions, embodies the presence of an individual who is admired, and acts as a bridge of familiarity connecting player and supporter. His note reading 'Up Cork, 1952' evokes a shared sentiment of well-wishes for the county. The train journey that permitted their interaction contrasts with the protocols and barriers that are now often present between teams and supporters on All-Ireland final day.

50. Gold Key from Opening of Casement Park (1953)

Cardinal Tomás Ó Fiaich Library, Armagh

When Casement Park, Belfast, opened in June 1953, it was the beginning of a new era for Gaelic games in Antrim and an impetus to other counties to provide similar facilities. The opening was marked with a day of activities, which were led by the Archbishop of Armagh, Cardinal John Dalton (1882–1963), who was presented with this engraved gold key to mark the occasion. A ticket cost ten shillings and admitted holders to the first match of the afternoon where All-Ireland hurling champions Cork played Galway. Later in the evening, a football match between Antrim and Kerry took place and tickets cost five shillings.

The ceremony, the naming of the stadium after an Irish patriot and the tricolour ticket were assertions and affirmations of an Irish nationalist identity, which was a reflection of the nature and ethos of the GAA at that time. Soil for the pitch was taken from Semple Stadium, Thurles and from Croke Park as a symbol of the unity of the GAA as a thirty-two-county organisation. The infrastructure came from repurposing materials from the surrounding areas. The main stand was built from reclaimed steel from abandoned American aircraft hangers sourced in Fermanagh, and household waste from the city's homes was piled up to create the hill on the Mooreland Park side. When the ground was finished, it became a sporting, cultural and social hub for the people of West Belfast and beyond. The stadium however, did not stand the test of time and due to local objections and political stalemates, it has lain idle and overgrown, with sporadic murmurings of it being returned to the days of glory and celebration that this gold key was designed to mark.

51. Miniature Sam Maguire Cup (1954)

GAA Museum, Croke Park

The holding aloft of the Sam Maguire Cup by a jubilant captain, surrounded by frenzied teammates and supporters, has become an iconic moment for the winners of the All-Ireland senior football championship since it was first presented in 1928. The cup is again the centre-point of celebrations which follow in the victorious county. As for the winning captains, they are each presented with a miniature replica of the Sam Maguire Cup. This miniature replica was presented to Meath's Peter McDermott (1918–2011), captain of the All-Ireland winning team in 1954. This was the eleventh miniature, with the first being presented after Roscommon's win in 1944. Similarly, the winning captains of the All-Ireland hurling championship receive a miniature of the Liam MacCarthy Cup.

There are many replicas of the Sam Maguire trophy, such as those presented to Club Person of the Year in Co. Longford; replicas made by silversmith George Bellew to celebrate the cup's jubilee in 1978; and Waterford Crystal replicas presented to commemorate seventy-five years of the Sam Maguire Cup in 2003. What distinguishes the captain's miniature from others is the engraving of the year, captain's name and county. In 1975, Kerry's Mickey O'Sullivan received his captain's miniature at a Central Council reception in Dublin the day after the final. Mickey missed out on the distinction of being presented with the Sam Maguire Cup itself on All-Ireland final day as he was severely concussed and rushed to hospital. When he eventually recovered almost an hour after the match, it was a nurse who informed him that Kerry had been victorious.

52. *Our Games* Annual (1958)

Private Collection (Jim Whelan, Graiguenamanagh)

Annuals as gift books originated in the early 19th century and experienced a boom in the 1930s. The GAA tapped into this lucrative Christmas market by publishing an annual gift book titled *Our Games*. Priced at ten shillings, the GAA's first annual appeared in time for Christmas 1958 and was published annually until 1979. Closely aligned with the design and style of other annuals at the time, the first 145-page annual contained a mix of stories, ballads, poems and quizzes in Irish and English. A review in Tipperary newspaper *The Nationalist* welcomed the publication and remarked that 'it is indeed time that we had such books to counteract the influence of foreign trash and rubbish, which finds its way into many Irish homes at Christmastide'.

As stated by General Secretary Pádraig Ó Caoimh in the introduction, the aim of the annual was to provide an image of Irish life as mirrored in the activities of the GAA. He also encouraged readers to share stories to pass onto the younger generation in which the humorous and the unique intermingle. In its early years, *Our Games* was primarily aimed at boys, with multiple reviews and advertisements remarking how it is 'a worthy annual for Irish boys and their fathers'. It then moved to be more inclusive and featured camogie and ladies football, as well as including colour photographs instead of black and white illustrations.

Publications dedicated to Gaelic games have appeared intermittently since the association's establishment, many of them short-lived. The first periodical was *The Celtic Times*, a newspaper co-edited by Michael Cusack and A. Morrison Millar that ran from 1 January 1887 to 14 January 1888. Others include the *Gaelic Weekly* newspaper, and the *Gaelic Sport*, *Hogan Stand* and *High Ball* magazines.

OUR
GAMES
ANNUAL

1958

Cumann Lúṫ-Ċleas Gaeḋeal
coisḋe connḋae Lonnḋain

Clár Oifigiúl

i bpáirc. Wembley

an 3.00 p.m.   16-5-59.

Cumann Lúiṫ

Éire

Cleas Gaeḋeal

peil: iomáint:
Gaillḃ   Cill Coinnig
     v   v
An Dún   Corcaiġ

Luaċ   Seán Ó Duinn,
1/-   Rúnái.

53. Wembley Match Programme (1959)

Private Collection (Jim Whelan, Graiguenamanagh)

One of the most ambitious undertakings of the London GAA county board came in 1957 when it booked Wembley Stadium for a festival of hurling and Gaelic football. At the time, the stadium had a capacity total of 100,000, with 40,000 of those in covered seated areas. The primary objective of the venture was to raise money to fund the London GAA's new grounds at New Eltham. This is the match programme from the Wembley GAA tournament which took place on 16 May 1959. Each province was represented as Galway played Down in football and Kilkenny played Cork in hurling.

The GAA in Britain had organised annual tournaments since the early 1920s in Mitcham Stadium in Surrey and at Woolwich and Herne Hill in the Greater London area. The largest attendance was in 1954 when 16,000 spectators watched Kerry play Armagh on Easter Monday. Despite the pitch at Wembley being approxi-mately ten yards short of the required playing area for Gaelic games, hosting GAA matches in such a distinguished venue was a determined statement of intent in promoting Gaelic games in Great Britain. The Irish diaspora in London was tasked with adorning dancehalls, churches, local shops and pubs with flyers advertising the event.

Although booked in 1957, the first tourna-ment did not take place until 1958 and it drew a crowd of over 33,000. Among those in attend-ance were London journalists, who described Gaelic football as 'a mixture between rugger and soccer' and hurling as 'hockey with the lid off' and 'legalised mayhem'. These tournaments took place annually at Wembley until 1976, when increasingly demanding intercounty schedules in Ireland meant that the interest in teams competing in additional competitions began to wane.

54. Hurl from Turloughmore's Six-in-a-row (*c.*1960s)

Seamus Murphy, Turloughmore

The 1960s were a golden era for hurling in Turloughmore, Co. Galway, which saw them capture six titles in a row in the senior club hurling championship from 1961 to 1966 – a feat never before or since accomplished in Galway hurling. Seamus Murphy played midfield for all six title wins and enjoyed a long hurling career that lasted well into the 1980s. He was one of only twenty-three players used in the six championships, which was a major factor in the team's success. This is one of the hurls that Seamus used during his long-standing career hurling with the club.

Hurling is deeply rooted in the parish of Turloughmore, with the GAA club founded at a meeting of the Irish National League in Lackagh National School in May 1886. In the early years of the GAA, Turloughmore became a central venue for many major tournaments and hosted the county senior football and hurling finals in 1896, which were played in the Fair Green. Turloughmore has a strong GAA history and this hurl helped to create that history.

The hurl, now well-weathered, has a worn black grip at the top of the handle with red and green tape below. There are three metal bands near the bas which mark where the hurl was repaired and re-banded on numerous occasions. Players of the modern game tend to opt for shorter hurls for more control and speed when rising the sliotar one-handed. This type of longer hurl is more conducive to ground hurling but is easier for the opposition to hook. Seamus remarks that the hurl is particularly heavy, but for the 100 games or more that he used it, it felt like part of his hand.

55. Co. Down Hand-knitted Cardigan (1960s)

Newry and Mourne Museum

On 22 September 1968, Down beat Kerry in the All-Ireland football final to bring Sam Maguire back to the Mourne county for the third time in nine years. A couple of days after the win, Down became the first Gaelic football team to receive a civic reception at Belfast City Hall and were feted throughout Ulster and their own county for months after. This hand-knitted jumper represents the romance and folklore that surrounded the Down teams of the 1960s.

Knitted by Philomena McGee from Carnmeen near Newry, the cream zip-up cardigan bears the design of footballers in the distinct red jersey and black shorts of Down. The cardigan is from a Mary Maxim graph-style knitting pattern, an American company which created the first easy-to-follow graph-style patterns. It is of the Cowichan style, which is a distinctly patterned design that originated in North America during the late 19th century among the Cowichan, a Coast Salish people in British Columbia. The cardigan was safeguarded in the family home until it was donated to the Newry and Mourne Museum in 2019.

The 1960s saw hand-knitted Irish goods ushered into an era of mass appeal, chiefly due to The Clancy Brothers, who were arguably Ireland's biggest cultural export of that decade and brought Aran sweaters to an international audience. Like Gaelic football, knitting is a craft that needs little equipment, a skill that can be passed down through generations and can function as a ritualising and rooting of relationships, traditions and places. This cardigan was created during Down's golden era of football and was knitted in Down by a woman who lived, worked and died in Down, giving the cardigan a distinct individuality and symbolic meaning.

56. Referee's Whistle (*c*.1960s)

Lár na Páirce, Thurles

Referees have ambitions of officiating significant matches but only a select few get the opportunity to be on the field on All-Ireland day. This is one of the whistles that Jimmy Hatton from Kilcoole, Co. Wicklow, used during his time as an intercounty referee. In 1966, Hatton achieved the rare record of refereeing both hurling and football finals in the same year. This made him only the third referee to officiate both senior finals, along with Jimmy Flaherty in 1939 and John Dowling in 1960, both from Tullamore, Co. Offaly. This distinct feat is likely to go unrepeated as the rules have since changed, stating that a referee can only officiate at one senior All-Ireland final in the same year. However, Hatton went one step further, as he also refereed the 1966 minor hurling final replay between Cork and Wexford, meaning that he refereed three All-Ireland finals that year.

This is an ACME thunderer whistle – the world's first specially manufactured sports whistle. First developed in the same year as the founding of the GAA, in 1884, this type of whistle is also known as the 'Titanic whistle', as it was used aboard the ill-fated vessel. This is a 'pea whistle', as the body of the whistle contains a 'pea' that moves with the airflow to produce its far-reaching sound across GAA pitches. The addition of the pea makes it possible to vary the sound produced by the whistle, making it a versatile tool of communication.

Hatton took up many roles within the GAA as player, referee, selector and treasurer. These roles often overlapped. In 1963, Hatton played at right half-back for the Wicklow hurlers in the Leinster junior hurling final versus Westmeath in Croke Park. Straight afterwards, he donned his referee gear and again took to the field, officiating the Kilkenny versus Dublin minor hurling semi-final. In 2005, Jimmy Hatton was inducted into the GAA Referees Hall of Fame.

57. All-Star Jersey (1963)

Galway City Museum

The first GAA All-Star awards were organised by the *Gaelic Weekly* newspaper and were presented in 1963. Judging panels were made up of journalists and former players. In addition, nomination papers were sent to every county chairman, allowing them to select players from each code. Fifteen players were selected on the All-Star hurling team, and fifteen for football, while one camogie player and one handballer were also honoured. The recipients gathered at a special banquet in the Gresham Hotel, Dublin, on 16 March, on the eve of the Railway Cup final. Instead of a trophy, the players each received a jersey with a star-shaped crest embroidered on it. This jersey, featuring the words 'Sár Peileadóir C.L.C.G. 1963', was presented to Galway's Pat Donnellan, who was selected at corner-forward on the 1963 All-Star football team.

Affectionately known as 'Pateen' among Galway supporters, Pat received a letter that he was being called up to the Galway senior football team in 1960, on the day he finished the last exam in his Leaving Certificate. He went on to have a successful intercounty career and was again selected on the All-Star team of 1966, this time in the midfield position. Pat shared much of his time playing for Galway with his brothers John and Michael. When Galway captured three-in-a-row All-Ireland titles in 1966, John captained the team.

The inaugural awards had one trophy – the Cú Chulainn award – presented to an individual who made an outstanding contribution to the GAA, which in 1963 was given to Pádraig Ó Caoimh, general secretary of the association. A formalised format of the GAA All-Stars was introduced in 1971, which was sponsored by tobacco firm PJ Carroll and Company and was the first high-profile commercial partnership entered into by the GAA.

58. Antrim Camogie Dress (*c*.1960s)

Private Collection (Bobby McIllhatton, Loughguile)

Tweed is an adaptable fabric that gives warmth and before the advance of high-performance textiles, it was considered the optimum textile for sports and outdoor wear. For this reason, it was used in GAA kits such as this Antrim camogie dress. This dress was worn with a dark belt across the waist and layered over a white short-sleeved blouse. It was handwoven by Glens of Antrim tweed, a small business which was based in a disused schoolhouse in Cushendall. Founded by John Denman Dean in 1964, he placed great importance on the training of local people by first-class designers and engineers. The business, which specialised in clothing, curtains and furnishing fabrics, was bombed in 1973 and went into receivership in 1980.

This dress was worn in the 1960s during a successful decade for Antrim camogie, in which they reached five All-Ireland senior finals, winning one title in 1967 after a replay versus Dublin. This win put a stop to Dublin's bid for eleven All-Ireland titles in a row. In a preview of the 1967 All-Ireland final, the *Evening Echo* reported that a win for Antrim 'would be a boost to all the other counties' as Dublin's dominance during this era caused 'many many players to become disheartened'.

Camogie uniforms, like much of the attire of female athletes, has a history of discomfort, with regulations and traditions being prioritised over athleticism. At the advent of camogie in the early 1900s, players wore full-length skirts and long-sleeved blouses. Gradually, skirt lengths began to rise and uniforms became less restrictive. There are now more options for camogie players when it comes to on-field style, including skorts, which comprise outer skirt and inner shorts, allowing for easy movement.

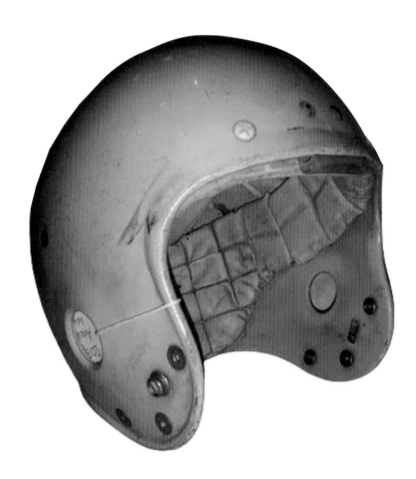

59. First GAA Helmet (1966)

GAA Museum, Croke Park

Although helmets were made compulsory for all players from 1 January 2010, their adoption as protective equipment was slow and reluctant in their early days. The widespread use of headgear for hurlers was first suggested by the University College Cork (UCC) club at the GAA Congress in 1968 and the college's hurlers have been pioneers when it comes to this, with many of their players being the first to wear helmets during different competitions. In the early 1940s, Derry Beckett wore a leather helmet similar to a rugby scrum cap during a Fitzgibbon Cup appearance, while Donal Clifford was the first to wear a helmet at inter-county level in the 1960s.

This helmet was worn by Micháel Murphy when he came on as a substitute in the Cork senior county final versus Avondhu in 1966. It is a motorcycle helmet cushioned inside for comfort, which had an elastic strap and chin pad. Helmets specially designed for hurling were first produced en masse in Ireland by William Cox (Ireland) Ltd – a plastic manufacturer in Clondalkin, Co. Dublin. Previous to this, helmets were imported from elsewhere and were designed for sports other than hurling.

Murphy endured a serious head injury during a championship match in 1964, which led him to advocate for protective headgear. It is perhaps no coincidence that the advent of helmets coincided with a serious injury on the biggest stage – the All-Ireland hurling final. In 1967, when Kilkenny took on Tipperary in the final, centre-forward Tommy Walsh received a hit which resulted in the loss of his left eye. He was forced to retire from hurling at the age of twenty-three and a fund was set up with clubs and county boards across the country contributing, especially in Tipperary. Walsh spent many years afterwards campaigning in schools about the importance of wearing adequate protective headgear.

60. Harty Cup Plaque (1967)

Limerick County Museum

In 1917, Dr John Harty (1867–1946), Archbishop of Cashel, offered a cup for a hurling competition between schools and colleges in Munster. The premise for this competition was to encourage Gaelic games in schools and to 'substitute Irish games in place of rugby and cricket as the chief games'. Limerick CBS enjoyed a successful period in the competition in the 1960s when they captured four Harty Cups in a row from 1964 to 1967. They were All-Ireland finalists in 1965 and 1967, and won the title in 1964 and 1966. This plaque was awarded to Tommy Keogh in recognition of his contribution as a member of the backroom team.

During the 1960s, the Harty Cup competition enjoyed widespread attention and thousands of supporters would cram into Harty Cup venues at Charleville, Buttevant and Clonmel, with special trains also provided to all three towns. At the Harty Cup final in 1964, when Limerick CBS took on St Flannan's College, Ennis, a record attendance of 11,000 was recorded. To escape the pre-match nerves ahead of the final, the team were taken by bus to Castleconnell that morning where they dined before returning to the city to the Ennis Road grounds. Reporting on that victory, the *Limerick Leader* newspaper remarked how their previous Harty Cup victory in 1932 sparked off 'the grandest ever Limerick hurling era – and is it too much to hope that the wonderful enthusiasm witnessed at the Gaelic Grounds will inspire the county to just another spell of equal significance.' As it happened, the school's success helped to lay the foundation for Limerick's All-Ireland glory in 1973, with several members of that Harty Cup team representing Limerick, including captain Éamonn Grimes.

61. Chalice with Football Medals (1968)

Augustinian Archives

From 1915 to 1918 the Wexford footballers held the title of All-Ireland champions, the first team to win four senior titles in a row. Aidan Doyle from New Ross featured in all four of these finals and was renowned for his versatility and ability to turn a game. He was a teenager when he won his first All-Ireland medal in 1915, scoring a goal in a match described at the time as 'the grandest exhibition of football that was ever played since the inception of the Association'.

In 1968, Aidan donated four of his medals to the Friary in New Ross, where he regularly attended 10 a.m. Mass. Two of these were his All-Ireland medals from 1915 and 1918, as well as a Leinster championship medal from 1913 and a division two junior football medal he won with Geraldine O'Hanrahans Club in 1919. It was decided that the medals would be fixed and bolted to the base of 'the best and most valuable chalice' in the Friary, which was a plain gold chalice. A written tribute to Aidan in the *New Ross Standard* after his death in 1977 advocated for those who see the chalice being used at Mass to 'offer a prayer for Aidan, and keep his name fresh and green in the county he loved and played for'.

The Augustinian Archives also hold a chalice which has Christy Ring's eighth All-Ireland hurling medal melted into it. Christy attended Mass regularly at Washington Street in Cork city and donated his treasured medal in 1954. In donating these much sought-after medals to the Augustinians to be repurposed in this way, Aidan Doyle and Christy Ring reinforced their personal identities as successful, record-setting GAA players and deeply devout religious people.

62. Letter from Fr Tom Scully to Offaly Footballers (1969)

Private Collection (O'Rourke Family, Killeigh)

Mick O'Rourke (1946–2019) played at corner-back for the Offaly footballers from 1968 to 1976. During his second season, he and his teammates received this letter from the manager, Fr Tom Scully (1930–2020), after their drawn game against Kildare in the National Football League. Possibly the equivalent of a group WhatsApp message today, the letter contains a response to criticism, an urging to protect the credibility of the team and a plea to foster a collective togetherness in being 'united and determined' to win. It also gives suggestions for training, diet and lifestyle.

Fr Scully took over as Offaly manager during a time of great optimism and expectation for the county. 1969 would be his only season as manager, but during his tenure he cultivated a close relationship with many of the players. Fr Scully was noted for his charisma, energy and positivity, which is evident in his words –

they capture a sense of urgency and belief that 'success is within grasp'. Through the 1960s, Fr Scully trained teams at colleges, junior and minor level, and during his time based at Belcamp College in Dublin, he held famously tough training sessions for any Offaly players living in the city.

The letter is dated 31 March 1969 (the day after the match took place) and permits access to the intimate sphere of team and management, including emotions, perceptions, criticisms and hope. The questions, warnings and motivational words in the letter were effective, as Offaly overcame Kildare in the replay on a scoreline of 1–2 to 0–8. The team would go on to the league final and All-Ireland final that year, losing both games to Kerry. Fr Scully's belief in his players was justified when, in 1971, they took All-Ireland honours, retaining the title the following year.

Belcamp College,

Dublin 5.

31st. March 1969.

Dear Player,

Last week we were written off as a useless team, not worth training. After last Sunday our supporters have warmed to us and are now telling us the great fellows we are. Be honest, have we proved we are great?? No. A drawn game is not a win, and Kildare have a great record for replays. So we must prove our worth by a good win over Kildare with our eyes set on League and All Ireland Honours. I think success is within grasp and appeal to each player to prepare himself to give his very best. One weakness on the team can and will be our downfall. Are you that weak link?? Are you prepared to train?? If not, at least be man enough and have the guts to resign from the panel of players. I want whole hearted, dedicated lads who will do themselves, the team and the County proud. There is no place for the shirker on our team.

Here are a few suggestions for training.

1. Train four or five days per week for about ½hour - or if you could manage it do ½hr. in morning and ½hr. at night. Beware of doing too much one day and then nothing for the rest of the week.

2. Training should be geared to give speed, stamina, and sharp reflexes - slow run, sprint, wlk, sprint, quick stop, left turn, right turn, reverse, sprint etc. etc. , all the time breathing deeply. If there is a good hill near you, use it; sprinting up and down a hill, forward and reverse will really strengthen your muscles.

3. Be careful of your diet, cut out rubbishy sweets etc. I recommend a raw egg and a glass of milk every day at 11.0.

4. Try to cut down on the smokes and drinks, and give yourself a chance by getting as much sleep as you can. Early nights much better than late mornings.

5. If there is no field or park near you, you can still train, if you want to, even in your flat. eg. a) On your toes for the 4 min. mile. b) Two minutes swinging left arm over right boot etc. c) 25 fast press-ups. d) Roll the body on the hips, lean back as far as possible and forward to touch the ground with closed fist, centre ,left and right. e) Lying on your back, hands smokinxy behind your head, raise your body to bring the head between the knees; balance on shoulder and neck , do the bicycle; flat on back lift legs slowly and controlled as high as possible, also slowly put one foot over the other slowly while keeping the feet only a few inches from the ground. Then lying on stomack raise head and legs about 13 inches off the ground.

Good luck and a happy Easter. United and determined we must win.

Yours   Tom Scully OMI.

T. Scully OMI

63. Handmade Model of GAA Pitch (*c*.1970s)

© National Museum of Ireland

Changes in the rules of the Gaelic games have largely dictated what GAA pitches have looked like. This handmade model of a GAA pitch shows that many changes have occurred to the specifications of the field of play. Donated to the National Museum of Ireland in 1972 by Killaloe native Michael Daly, it is not known when it was made, but its measurements and specifications predate 1910 due to the presence of two outer posts on either side of the goal, similar to International Rules. Any score outside of the goal area but between these outer posts was worth one point.

When the GAA was first formed, pitch markings were casually implemented, if at all. Pitches during the formative years of the GAA were patches of grass wherever they could be found. The 1893 All-Ireland finals were due to take place in Ashtown, Co. Dublin, but playing conditions were deemed unsuitable as there were no pitch markings, and the grass was knee-high and bedecked with haystacks. The games were relocated to the nearby Phoenix Park, where the Wexford footballers and Cork hurlers emerged victorious.

When Gaelic games became more established and more clubs had their own pitches, proper pitch markings were laid down. This coincided with the rules becoming more official and the quality of pitches – and indeed play – reflecting that. The first GAA rules written in 1885 had different pitch specifications for hurling and football, with the dimensions for hurling pitches much larger. This model shows that the pitch is 196 yards long and 100 yards across, which is closer to the early dimensions used for hurling. Other notable changes to GAA pitches include the introduction of the parallelogram at the 21-yard line in 1910, and the pushing of penalties further from the target when measurements changed from the imperial to the metric system in 1978.

64. Scór Programme (1973)

Fermanagh County Museum Collection, Museum Services,
Fermanagh & Omagh District Council

Scór officially became an integral part of the GAA in 1970 when a motion was passed at the GAA Congress for a national competition at youth and adult levels that actively supported the Irish language, traditional Irish dancing, music, song and other aspects of Irish culture. Scór was initially the concept of Derry Gowen (1933–2017), who founded Scór in north Cork in 1969, was the first chairman of the National Committee of Scór and compiled the first rules for the competition. The competition uses the ready-made structures of the GAA club championships, with clubs competing against each other first within the county before qualifying for the provincial and All-Ireland finals.

This programme is from the Fermanagh Scór finals in 1973, which took place in the Astral Cinema in Lisnaskea. It lists the competitors in each of the eight categories: solo dance, solo song, recitation, novelty act, quiz, instrumental music, set dancing and ballad group. The programme has handwritten notes which list the songs and tunes performed. The Scór rules for ballad groups stipulate that they must sing ballads of the history of Ireland, its people, places and folklore. In this instance, the songs include many that capture and support the political ideals of those who sought an independent Ireland, including 'Only Our Rivers Run Free', 'Boys of the Old Brigade' and 'Jim Larkin'.

Scór competitions are divided into two age levels: Scór na nÓg, for young people under seventeen and Scór Sinsir, for those over seventeen. All-Ireland Scór winners are presented with their medals by the president of the GAA, in the same way as any All-Ireland GAA champions.

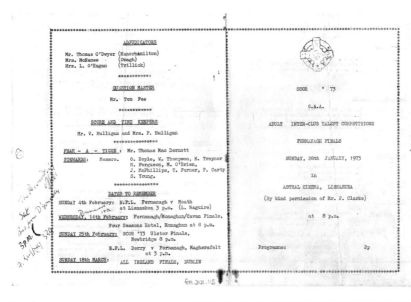

ADJUDICATORS

Mr. Thomas O'Dwyer (Manorhamilton)
Mrs. McManee   (Omagh)
Mrs. L. O'Hagan   (Trillick)

****

QUESTION MASTER

Mr. Tom Fee

****

SCORE AND TIME KEEPERS:

Mr. V. Mulligan and Mrs. F. Mulligan

****

FEAR - A - TIGHE : Mr. Thomas Mac Dermott

STEWARDS: Messrs.   O. Boyle, W. Thompson, E. Traynor
                      H. Ferguson, M. O'Brien,
                      J. McPhillips, T. Farmer, P. Carty
                      S. Young.

DATES TO REMEMBER

SUNDAY 4th February: N.F.L. Fermanagh v Meath
                     at Lisnaskea 3 p.m. (L. Maguire)
WEDNESDAY, 14th February: Fermanagh/Monaghan/Cavan Finals,
                     Four Seasons Hotel, Monaghan at 8 p.m.
SUNDAY 25th February: SCOR '73 Ulster Finals,
                     Newbridge 8 p.m.

                     N.F.L. Derry v Fermanagh, Magherafelt
                     at 3 p.m.
SUNDAY 18th MARCH: ALL IRELAND FINALS, DUBLIN

SCOR ' 73

G.A.A.

ADULT INTER-CLUB TALENT COMPETITIONS

FERMANAGH FINALS

SUNDAY, 28th JANUARY, 1973

in

ASTRAL CINEMA, LISNASKEA

(By kind permission of Mr. F. Clarke)

at 8 p.m.

Programme: 2p

PART ONE

SOLO DANCE:

1. Mrs. Curran (Brookeboro)
2. Ursuala Gaffney (Derrygonnelly)
3. Maureen O'Brien (Belnaleck)

****

SOLO SONG OR BALLAD:

1. Mrs. Noreen Donnelly (Lisbellaw)
2. Des Hynes (Enniskillen Gaels)
3. John Murphy (Brookeboro)
4. Kathleen McKeaney (Derrygonnelly)

****

RECITATION:

1. Hugh Cox (Lisbellaw)
2. Marie McKenna (Roslea)
3. Celine McPartland (Belcoo)

****

NOVELTY ACT:

1. Brookeboro (Home Cooking)
   John Murphy, Mrs. Agnes Lavery,
   Mrs. Moira Leonard.

2. Derrygonnelly (Mistaken Identity)

   Patsy Burns, Bernadette Burns,
   Eamon Greene.

PART TWO

QUESTION TIME: 1. Lisbellaw (Mick Murphy, Hugh Cox, Eamon
                   Donnelly)
                2. Enniskillen Gaels (Tom Keavney, Paddy
                   Moore, Brendan
                   Mc Manus.
                3. Aghadrumsee (Jimmy Quinn, Jim McCaul,
                   John O'Hara)
                4. Erne Gaels (Seamus Heron, Charlie Cullen,
                   Jim Flanagan)

****

INSTRUMENTAL MUSIC: 1. Hugh Cox (Lisbellaw) Tin Whistle
                     2. Frank Murphy (Brookeboro) Accordeon
                     3. Mick Hoy (Derrygonnelly) Violin
                     4. J. Maguire (Belnaleck) Accordeon

SET DANCING: 1. Aghadrumsee (Mr. & Mrs. E. McMahon,
                 Mrs. Durnian, Phil Scott

              2. Belcoo Group

BALLAD GROUPS:

1. Enniskillen Gaels: (Roisin & Niní
   McElhill, Mary Herbert, Sean O'Hare
   Seamus Faulkner)
2. Roslea: (Gerard McMahon, Mary McCaffrey,
   Anne Callaghan, Gerard Slowey)
3. Derrygonnelly Rovers:
   Kathleen McKeaney, Rose McKeaney
   Jim McGrath, Phil Love,
   Jim McCarron.
4. Lisbellaw Mise Eire (Gabriel Quinn,
   Marian McKeogh, Mary McCarney,
   Veronica O'Connor, G. O'Connor.

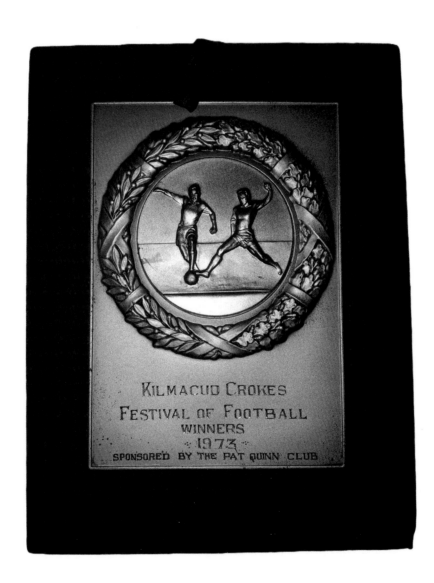

KILMACUD CROKES
FESTIVAL OF FOOTBALL
WINNERS
·1973·
SPONSORED BY THE PAT QUINN CLUB

65. Kilmacud Sevens Winners Plaque (1973)

Private Collection (Tom Hunt, Mullingar)

In 1919, the Kilmacud GAA tournament was played with the objective of strengthening the coal fund for the deserving poor of the Stillorgan district in Dublin. This set the precedent for the first annual Kilmacud hurling sevens tournament in 1959, which was followed in 1973 by a football tournament and later the incorporation of a camogie competition. This plaque was won by Tom Hunt, a member of the University College Dublin (UCD) team which was victorious in the inaugural football tournament. UCD beat Shannon Rangers in the final and was managed by GAA journalist and intercounty manager Eugene McGee (1941–2019). A notable feature of the 1973 tournament was that players from the civil service camogie club were sideline officials.

The Kilmacud sevens tournament is held annually on the same weekend as the All-Ireland finals and has become an integral part of the match build-up. As well as being a social event, it is also renowned as the place to source an elusive All-Ireland ticket. Club teams qualify by winning their county championship and also by invitation. For the 40th anniversary tournament, all previous winners were invited back, and in 2013, a team of Dáil Éireann 'All Stars' took on a GAA media selection. Many annual sevens tournaments have followed, including those organised by Monaghan Harps ladies football and West Coast Sevens in San Diego each May; they are generally played on a pitch of a reduced size and an abridged playing time of 15 minutes per half in a round robin format.

66. Joe Kernan's Runners-up Plaque (1977)

Private Collection (Joe Kernan, Crossmaglen)

In 1977, Armagh played Dublin in the All-Ireland senior football final, with Dublin prevailing on a scoreline of 5–12 to 3–6. Scoring two of Armagh's goals that day was midfielder Joe Kernan. This was Armagh's last appearance in an All-Ireland final until they played Kerry in the 2002 final. Joe was once again instrumental in that significant moment in Armagh GAA history, but this time as manager of the team.

Trailing favourites Kerry by four points at half-time, Joe addressed his players in the dressing room and implored that they should not settle for second best. To emphasise his point further, Joe produced this plaque that he and each of his teammates were presented with as runners-up of the 1977 All-Ireland final. The plaque is a possession that Joe was somewhat ashamed of and had hidden away because he perceived it as a symbol of losing, rather than its original intention of marking the

achievement of reaching an All-Ireland final. In the dressing room, Joe held up the plaque, showed it to his players and asked, 'Do you want one of these?' That plaque, he said, was the sign of a loser and he didn't want the team to have to endure the same emotions he had for all those years. He then smashed it off the wall with major dramatic effect and broke it. The plaque had a medal nailed to it, which also broke off in the process.

Joe's use of this plaque as a prop during his half-time speech proved to be appropriate motivation for his players and they confined their Kerry opponents to three points during the second half. As Joe watched Armagh win their first All-Ireland senior title that day, the plaque lay broken on the dressing room floor. It remains in two fragments, with the medal detached, as a symbol of Joe's emotion and passion for Armagh football.

67. Dóirín Mhic Mhurchú's Handmade Press Pass (1970s)

Clann Mhic Mhurchú, An Rinn, Co. Phortláirge

When Raidió na Gaeltachta began broadcasting from its main studio at Casla in Connemara on Easter Sunday, 2 April 1972, it made a significant contribution to the sustainability and development of the Irish language. Dóirín Mhic Mhurchú (1930–2014) was the station's first and only female sports reporter. Travelling to GAA matches on her Honda 50, Dóirín spent forty years providing match reports and content for the radio station. She would relay the match results to Spórt an Domhnaigh by phone and signed off each of her match reports with the words 'Dóirín Mhic Mhurchú anso, sa Rinn'.

Dóirín's entry into sports broadcasting was not without its obstacles, and in one instance she was initially refused entry to the media box at Semple Stadium, Thurles. The steward on duty, believing that she had found herself in the press box by accident, said, 'Sorry, Ma'am, these seats are for the Press', which was met by her defiant reply: 'I am the Press!' This prompted Dóirín to make her own press card for identification as she awaited the arrival of her official National Union of Journalists card. Using Pritt Stick and a piece of cardboard, she pasted the Raidió na Gaeltachta logo and contact details on one side and, on the other side, she stuck the word 'Press', cut from an edition of *The Irish Press*. This makeshift press pass sufficed as proof of her credentials and has been kept by her family as a reminder of the barriers that she had to overcome to make her own special mark in GAA broadcasting.

Dóirín's involvement in GAA and Irish culture was varied and far-reaching. When the GAA launched a campaign to promote the Irish language, she was the only female Irish language officer in the country. As well as being an accomplished journalist, musician and poet, Dóirín won a Waterford Junior Camogie Championship title in 1974, playing alongside her daughter Áine, with her grandchild watching from the sideline.

68. John Egan's Glove (1978)

Cardinal Tomás Ó Fiaich Library, Armagh

John Egan (1952–2012) first played football for the Kerry senior team in 1972. He went on to play in eight All-Ireland senior football finals, winning six of them. This is one of the gloves that he wore in the 1978 All-Ireland football final versus Dublin, during which he scored 1–2 as the Kerry team began a four-in-a-row title sequence.

Because this type of glove was designed for warmth, they were not very functional in terms of catching and carrying a football but were important for blood circulation. But the development of football gloves accelerated and they soon evolved in both style and substance; by the time Egan captained Kerry in the 1982 final, he had upgraded to gloves with added padding. That year, Kerry were bidding for a historic five-in-a-row titles but succumbed to Seamus Darby and Offaly in one of the most celebrated and dramatic All-Ireland finals of all time.

The 1978 All-Ireland final is probably most famous for a bizarre and contentious goal scored by Mikey Sheehy. As the Dublin goalkeeper, Paddy Cullen, was arguing with the referee over a free that was awarded to Kerry, the ball was chipped over his head and into the net before he could return to guard it. Although Kerry went on to be emphatic winners that day on a scoreline of 5–11 to 0–9, the legitimacy of the goal has been widely debated because of the difficulty in seeing where the foul was committed in the first place. Referee Seamus Aldridge maintains that if he had the chance to reconsider the decision, he would not award the free 'as it would save him a lot of hassle'. Aldridge was subjected to abuse from agitated supporters, one of whom sent him a bullet in the post, and for ten years after the match he received phone calls, sometimes at 3 a.m., contesting that very free.

69. Poc Fada Marking Stone (*c.*1980s)

Cooley Mountains, Co. Louth

Walk up the stony terrain of the Cooley Mountains at Annaverna and you will find a dolmen and two yellow-painted upright standing stones. The stones are purposely placed and mark the start and finish point for the All-Ireland Poc Fada competition – an annual national contest for hurlers and camogie players. The objective is to puck a sliotar as far as possible and to get around the mountain in the fewest possible number of shots. The route is marked by dozens of these yellow-painted stones that indicate the 5km circuit. Initially, the standing stones were painted white, but from a distance local farmers mistook them for sheep, so it was decided to paint the stones yellow. This standing stone has 'An Poc Fada' engraved into it and an arrow pointing towards the direction to take along the circuit.

The first Poc Fada competition ran in 1960 and, following this, usually took place on the seventh Sunday after Easter, a day known as Whit Sunday, traditionally regarded in Ireland as a 'fatal and unlucky time'. Thought to be the unluckiest day of the year, people were encouraged to stay indoors, and because of this, hurling and football matches did not take place on Whit Sunday. However, the Poc Fada competition prevailed and the freeing-up of the fixtures schedule on that Sunday allowed hurlers to compete, many of whom were intercounty goalkeepers.

The competition was suspended in 1970 due to a lack of entries but was later revived in 1981 on a new course. The course has four stages with three turning points – An Céide, Carn an Mhadaigh and An Gabhlan – as well as the added challenge of crossing a ravine on the last leg. In a time when Gaelic games are subject to constant changes in rules, equipment and tactics, Poc Fada has retained its steady, uncomplicated form within the wild foothills of Co. Louth.

70. Prison Art from Long Kesh (1980s)

National Museums Northern Ireland

Long Kesh prison, near Lisburn, Co. Down, is one of the primary sites associated with the Troubles in Northern Ireland (1968–1998). This wooden shield with hurls and sliotar was made by a member of the IRA's D Company while interned there. A harp rests in the centre of the shield, made of pieces of coloured plastic and stick on gems. Arts and crafts were pursued at an informal level within Long Kesh, but classes were also held as part of educational programmes.

In 1980, when IRA prisoners at Long Kesh were first contemplating hunger strikes as a protest strategy against the prison conditions, they were appealing to nationalist Ireland to show support for their campaign and saw the GAA as being integral to this. Prisoners pleaded with the GAA and local clubs to issue statements in support of them and also for members to take part in marches. Perhaps the creation of this artwork that incorporates symbols of Gaelic games was an attempt to visualise that campaign.

The Troubles exposed the contradiction of the GAA identifying as a nationalist but non-political organisation, because in Northern Ireland, nationalism was and is invariably political. A ban prohibited prisoners from playing Gaelic games in Long Kesh, and at the Tyrone county convention in 1984, the Carrickmore and Castlederg clubs put forward a motion that the association act immediately to ensure the ban was lifted. The governing bodies of the GAA were encouraged to publicly support the aims of political prisoners but declined, demonstrating the association's complex relationship with Irish nationalism and republicanism.

71. *Up for the Final* Concert Programme (1982)

Cardinal Tomás Ó Fiaich Library, Armagh

All-Ireland final weekend brings an atmosphere of excitement and expectation. Sometimes the excitement unfolds in advance of the final as supporters can get great enjoyment from expanding expectations in the hours leading up to the match itself. A céilí in the Mansion House in Dublin city was the traditional social event the night before the All-Ireland final. This changed in 1982, when a concert took place in the RDS in front of an audience of 4,000 and was broadcast live on RTÉ One.

This programme is for the first *Up for the Final* concert on the eve of the 1982 hurling final between Cork and Kilkenny. The concert was presented by broadcaster Donncha Ó Dúlaing (1933–2021) and featured performances by Larry Cunningham and The Wolfe Tones. The event brought together a blend of conversation, entertainment and music, allowing viewers to capture the anticipated drama of the All-Ireland final based on shared memories and entertainment. This was followed by another concert in the National Stadium with an audience of 5,000 ahead of the football final two weeks later.

The concert took place in the hope that it would become an annual event 'for which tickets will have to be allocated in much the same way as they are for the All-Ireland hurling and football finals'. That hope was realised and it later became known as *Up for the Match*. There were, however, mixed reactions to that first concert when it was broadcast. John Cunningham, writing for the *Connacht Sentinel* newspaper, criticised the sound quality, blasted the production as 'the most sloppy job in television' and described the staging as 'about as well constructed as those alleged toilets which the GAA provides in country grounds'. Nevertheless, the premise of the programme has stood the test of time and demonstrates how the excitement of All-Ireland finals need not be confined to the stadium.

72. Centenary Cairn (1984)

Kilclief Ben Dearg GAC

Stone cairns have been built since prehistoric times and are used across many different cultures as landmarks, burial sites and trail markers. This stone cairn was built on the grounds of Kilclief Ben Dearg GAC (Gaelic Athletic Club), Co. Down, to commemorate the GAA's centenary in 1984. Created by local craftsmen James Denvir and Patsy King, it comprises stones from every townland, mass site and former GAA pitch in the parish of Kilclief. The cairn was unveiled by Fr Kelly, parish priest and president of the club on 28 July 1984. This date was designated by the GAA for each club around the country to organise special celebrations to mark the centenary of the association.

The idea for Kilclief Ben Dearg's Lá na gClub was not to focus on past achievements, but to look to future generations. With this in mind, a time capsule was buried underneath the cairn, which contained photographs of teams, newspapers and details of the centenary celebrations. The instruction is that in 2034, the time capsule will be opened to coincide with the GAA's 150th anniversary and fifty years since the time capsule and cairn were put in place.

Kilclief is located on the edge of Co. Down's eastern coast, in a small area where the Isle of Man is visible in the distance on a clear day. In the club's early years, its teams played on many different pitches throughout the parish, but in the 1950s they settled in the present location – St Malachy's Park on the banks of Strangford Lough. During building works on the grounds in recent years to update the facilities and to create a community walkway, the cairn was moved but remained completely intact, with the time capsule undisturbed.

FOOT BALL
CLUB
NEW YORK CITY

July 27–August 11th
1984
To celebrate
the Centennial
of the
Gaelic Athletic
Association

73. 'Donegal Goes Home' Centennial Poster (1984)
Donegal Archives

The Irish diaspora played an integral role in the GAA's centenary celebrations in 1984, with many taking the opportunity to join in the celebrations in Ireland. One of the teams to travel to Ireland during the centenary year was Donegal New York GAA team. The official travelling party during their two-week tour of Donegal comprised fifty-five members. This poster, in Celtic-style typeface, promoted the tour, which was planned over a year in advance, with meetings and newspaper notices inviting clubs wishing to be involved to get in touch.

The Donegal New York team spent their tour being welcomed by various GAA clubs and dignitaries, parading around the county alongside local bands, and attending functions where medals were presented and gifts exchanged. They also had a busy schedule of football matches against Gweedore, Sean MacCumhaills, Carndonagh, Urris, Ardara and Tir Chonaill Gaels of London, all of whom they defeated. The only team to emerge

victorious versus Donegal New York on the tour was Kilcar, on a scoreline of 1–7 to 0–9. The Letterkenny leg of the tour was labelled 'an embarrassment' in the *Donegal News* due to the conspicuous absence of club mentors, players and members. It was also reported that St Eunan's Club's activities for the centenary, which included Lá na gClub and Féile na Gaeilge, were poorly supported.

Despite this, one of the highlights of the 'Donegal Goes Home' tour was the travelling party's attendance at the final of the Mary From Dungloe Festival, which is centred around a competition to find the woman who best embodies 'the spirit of the festival'; she is then crowned 'Mary From Dungloe'. In a fitting (or questionable) result, with such a strong contingent from New York in attendance, the winner in 1984 was the New York contestant, Anne Marie Maloney. Newspapers reported how 'all hell broke loose' with excitement when she was selected.

74. Sculpture Presented to Michael O'Hehir (1988)

Private Collection (O'Hehir Family)

Michael O'Hehir (1920–1996) was a broadcaster and journalist who gave his first commentary on a GAA match at the age of eighteen in 1938, when Galway defeated Monaghan in the All-Ireland football semi-final in Cusack Park, Co. Westmeath. He went on to have a successful career providing vivid accounts of Gaelic games, boxing, showjumping and horse racing for radio listeners. Michael commentated on ninety-nine All-Ireland finals in all codes, including several replays, until his retirement in 1985. This sculpture was presented to him by Bank of Ireland at the 1988 All-Star awards to mark his successful broadcasting career and his association with the All-Stars as a selector since their inception. The sculpture is specially designed to represent Michael's commentary, with a microphone on the bottom and the figure on top portraying both hurling and Gaelic football. It is in the same style as the sculptures given to the All-Stars of that era, which were created by Dublin-born sculptor Rowan Gillespie.

Michael's parents were both from Clare and he grew up in Drumcondra near Croke Park, where he would later spend many weekends bringing matches to life. It was a strong GAA household; his father, Jim, was trainer of the Clare hurling team who won the 1914 All-Ireland hurling title and also of the Leitrim football team who won the Connacht championship in 1927.

The technology of radio changed the way sport and Gaelic games were experienced by those who could not attend the events in person. The accessibility of live radio coverage and Michael's commentary generated the tension and excitement of actual attendance and increased the GAA's popularity. With his microphone always in his right hand and a stopwatch in his left, Michael brought the drama of Gaelic games into many homes in his compelling and recognisable style, which transcended the generations.

75. Trevor Giles's Sleeveless Jersey (1990s)

GAA Museum, Croke Park (on loan from Trevor Giles)

The summer of 1999 saw Meath's Trevor Giles make a noticeable alteration to his jersey by cutting off most of the sleeves. The DIY aero-dynamic jersey alleviated heat for the centre-forward during a season in which Meath prevailed as All-Ireland senior football champions. This look may have been influenced by his time playing for Ireland in the International Rules series versus Australia. Australian players wear jerseys with cap sleeves – not only to reduce heat, but to stop their markers having something substantial to grab on to.

In order to meet the demands of an increasingly competitive sport, GAA jerseys have become more functional and have moved from heavy woollen pullovers to more breathable materials that can moderate a player's body temperature, thus ensuring optimal performance. There are no rules against making adjustments to jerseys, but there are strict guidelines around sponsors and the positioning of logos. In 2021, the GAA granted permission to allow sponsorship on the sleeves of player and replica jerseys, so it is likely that Giles's adjustment would not stand up under current rules.

GAA jerseys symbolise membership of a group, while creating exclusion and otherness to people outside of that group. They also create team spirit, brand identity and enthusiasm among players and supporters. Given that GAA players are most often seen and not heard during their playing careers, clothing can be an important means of self-presentation during their time in the spotlight. In an environment where uniformity is expected and much emphasis is put on the pride of the jersey, Giles used his now iconic jersey as a tool for self-expression.

76. Donegal Champions Jigsaw (1993)

Cardinal Tomás Ó Fiaich Library, Armagh

The market and variety of GAA merchandise is constantly expanding and evolving. From handmade headbands for sale outside stadium grounds to mass-produced teddy bears wearing team colours, merchandise can bring the visibility of Gaelic games to consumers and to outside observers. The consumption of such products is often increased by a team's success and when Donegal won their first All-Ireland senior football title in 1992, it prompted a surge in merchandise, such as this 500-piece commemorative jigsaw. It was produced by Stewart Puzzles in Clarcam, Co. Donegal and was sold at a price of £6.50.

There are strict rules around the use of the official GAA logo and county crests in order to protect the integrity of the association and its branding. Neither features on this jigsaw as it is not an official GAA product. Despite their omission, the jigsaw triggers responses of immediate recognition with the dominant green and gold of Donegal and the familiar format of the pre-match team photo on All-Ireland final day. The jigsaw features an alternate crest, which has minor adjustments to avoid breaching any copyright or branding rules. The hand of King Conall's cross is on the opposite side to the official crest and notably, there is no mention of GAA on the product itself. Instead, the side of the box is filled with generic but GAA-related sayings such as 'Sam for the Hills' and ''92-DL-SAM'.

Champions

Back Row, left to right: Martin Shovlin, Paul Callaghan, John Joe Doherty, Matt Gallagher, Noel Hegarty, Gary Walsh, Brian Murray, Barry McGowan, Declan Bonner, Donal Reid, Barry Cunningham.
Middle Row, left to right: Paul Carr, Sylvester McGuire, Martin McHugh, Joyce McMullan, Manus Boyle, Tony Boyle, Anthony Molloy, Martin Gavigan, James McHugh, John Cunningham.
Front Row, left to right: Jim McGuinness, Charlie Mulgrew, Michael Gallagher, Mark Crossan, Tommy Ryan.

Photo by Declan Doherty

Donegal

77. 'Dancing at the Crossroads' Cassette (1996)

Private Collection (Darcy Family, Ballyhogue)

In 1996, the Wexford hurlers captured the Liam MacCarthy Cup for the first time since 1968. Their championship journey in beating Kilkenny, Offaly, Galway and Limerick was set to the soundtrack of The Wild Swans, a duo made up of Brendan Wade and Paul Bell. The upbeat song 'Dancing at the Crossroads' captures the excitement of All-Ireland glory and the lyrics list the names of the 1996 Wexford hurling squad. The B-side to the song was 'The Purple and Gold', an emotive ballad that tells the story of the pride and privilege of supporting Wexford.

Music is used to enhance GAA events in many ways, such as anthems, chants, theme tunes and intermission entertainment. Many artists have penned GAA songs and it is an especially busy market in the lead up to All-Ireland finals. A victory is a sure-fire way of a song gaining popularity and extending its life cycle. The Wild Swans gained nationwide popularity after the Model County's win, and 'Dancing at the Crossroads' reached number one in the Irish charts, knocking the Spice Girls' 'Wannabe' off the top spot that September. This was an extraordinary feat given that the single was initially only available on cassette during a time when technology was rapidly advancing towards CDs.

'Dancing at the Crossroads' is still played in many pubs and venues, especially during the GAA season. In 2014, P.J. O'Brien's, an Irish pub in Sydney, removed 'Dancing at the Crossroads' from their jukebox due to the boisterous behaviour that it caused whenever it was played. Petitions were created on social media and the song was soon reinstated to the pub jukebox, demonstrating how it continues to inspire a state of excitement and nostalgia for a special time in Wexford GAA history.

78. Colie K's Hole in the Ceiling (1998)

Taaffes Bar, Galway City

In 1998, the Galway footballers won the All-Ireland senior championship for the eighth time in the county's history. While almost 71,000 spectators were in attendance at Croke Park that day to see Galway take on Kildare, many more watched the game from homes and venues the world over. One of them was Colie K, who worked as a barman in Taaffes Bar in Galway city – an establishment which has seen many Galway players pass through as employees. Bar manager Pádraig Lally, whose family own the pub, was part of the Galway team who captured the Sam Maguire in 2001.

Four minutes into the second half of the 1998 final, full-forward Pádraic Joyce split the defence to score a goal that shifted the balance of power in the game. As the goal hit the back of the net, Colie jumped with excitement, struck the ceiling above the bar with his fist and burst a hole in it. Instead of repairing the hole, it was framed as a reminder of that famous day in Galway football.

Pubs play an important role in Gaelic games – as meeting points for discussions, as part of match-day routines and as a post-match outlet for supporters and players alike. Pubs are embraced as an alternative site for viewing matches, and they bring a party atmosphere just like the stadium, along with all the stress and excitement of a live match. Often, a spectator's need for proximity is not for proximity to the match itself, but to the atmosphere and social interaction that sport brings. That day, Colie K and Pádraic Joyce celebrated in sync with each other – one of them punching the ceiling of a pub in Galway, the other punching the air in front of Galway supporters on Hill 16.

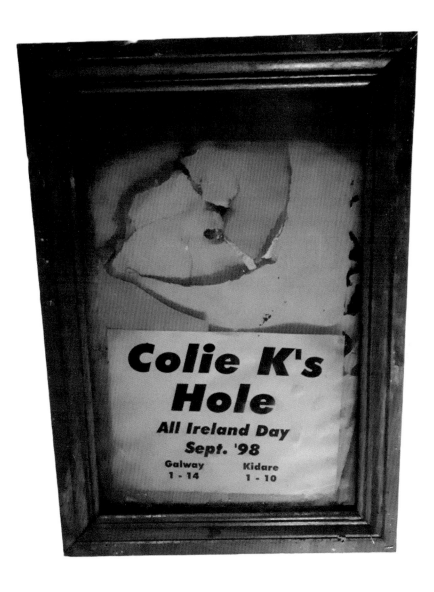

79. 'John 3:7' Sign (1999)

This sign will be familiar to many GAA fans as it has been present at many GAA matches and spotted by observant TV viewers. Its bearer, Frank Hogan (1938–2020), positioned himself behind the goal on Hill 16 and in various venues across the country. Originally from Borrisokane, Co. Tipperary, Frank made his home in Castletroy and followed Limerick for over three decades, carrying one of these signs with him to GAA matches of all codes. Here, Frank holds up his sign in the Gaelic Grounds in Limerick while watching the National Hurling League Division 1 semi-final between Kilkenny and Galway in 1999.

Frank's inspiration for the sign came after he noticed one of similar design in the crowd as tennis player Pat Cash was presented with the trophy after winning the men's singles tournament at Wimbledon in 1987. That sign was considerably smaller than Frank's and read 'John 3:16' which refers to a verse from the Bible. Frank adopted this for some time, as he hoped to spread a Christian message, but found that the verse was too long for him to recite when people inquired as to its meaning. He then reverted to 'John 3:7', which reads: 'Do not marvel that I said to you, you must be born again'.

The sign, which is printed in black letters on a bright yellow background and with a wooden frame surrounding it, was understandably awkward for Frank to carry to and from matches, but he always persevered. In 2009, as Frank made his way home from attending a match in Croke Park, the sign was stolen on the train journey back to Limerick. It later mysteriously appeared at Kildare Garda Station a few days later and was front-page news when it was returned. Frank's trips around the country with his iconic sign were not confined to GAA matches and also included visits to the Rose of Tralee festival, the Galway Races, fleadhanna and music concerts.

80. Shane Curran's Kicking Tee (*c.*2000s)

Private Collection (Shane Curran, Co. Roscommon)

Gaelic games require innovation that gives players marginal gains and influences how the game is played. This can come in the form of tactics, training and physical conditioning but also in the form of equipment used. This kicking tee was used by Roscommon and St Brigid's goalkeeper Shane Curran, who was one of the first goalkeepers to take long-range frees. Using bristles which give the impression of kicking off grass, it assists with longer and more accurate kickouts and reduces the risk of injury.

To support the position of the ball when taking kickouts, many players would gouge sods from the ground at the expense of the pristine surface so carefully maintained by groundskeepers. Shane's first kicking tee was an improvised one that he made by cutting the bottom off a large plastic bottle. Seeing the potential and necessity for such a product, he worked to develop a kicking tee specifically for Gaelic football. When they were formally introduced in 2005, some goalkeepers expressed reservations because of the impact it has on the facility to take a quick kick-out. However, there has since been a notable difference in the length and height of kickouts, as well as a better standard of fielding.

The role of goalkeeper in Gaelic football is one which has changed considerably in recent years. Analysis and an increase in the usage of data has played a part, but the value and importance of kickouts has had an immense effect on the reliance on goalkeepers. Retention of the ball is crucial, so there is increased pressure on goalkeepers in maintaining accuracy with their kickouts, underlining the impact of the kicking tee in training and competition.

81. Anthony Tohill's Football Boots (2001)

Derry City & Strabane District Council Museum & Heritage Service Collections

Most GAA players specialise in their sport of choice; some are dual players, but few transition to other sports at an elite level. Anthony Tohill is best known as a midfielder for Swatragh and Derry, but he also gained recognition in soccer, the Australian Football League (AFL) and International Rules. In August 2001, Tohill wore these football boots in the All-Ireland semi-final versus Galway at Croke Park. Two months later, he wore them in Melbourne as Ireland captain in the International Rules series against Australia.

In 1990, Tohill was recruited from the junior Gaelic football ranks in Derry and spent time in Melbourne playing for the Demons club in the AFL. A year later, he returned to Ireland and went straight into the senior team in Derry, a team he would win a coveted All-Ireland medal with in 1993. Tohill also spent some time playing soccer with Derry City and in 1995, he played with the Manchester United reserves during a two-week trial with the club. Tohill finished his soccer trial on a Wednesday night and by Sunday he was back on the Derry panel for a national league game versus Down. He had a long and successful period with the Ireland team in the International Rules series as a player, captain and manager.

These are Adidas Predator Precision boots, which launched in 2000 and were revolutionary in their technology. They feature Traxion studs, which allowed Tohill to adjust the boots to certain pitch conditions. The foldover tongue is embroidered with 'Doire', an identity marker and communication tool for Tohill to tell the world where he was from. The customisation, made in the penultimate year of his playing career, represents Tohill adding a layer of subtle difference that signified his rise through the ranks from substitute to captain of his county and country.

82. Kit Manager's Bag (2003)

Private Collection (Tommy Murphy, Kildare)

In 2003, the Kildare footballers played Laois in the Leinster senior football final, which at the time was a highly anticipated fixture as Laois manager Mick O'Dwyer had previously managed Kildare. That day Laois came out as winners, capturing their first Leinster title since 1946. In the Kildare dressing room and on the sideline was kit manager Tommy Murphy. His role, and the role of the many people who manage team kits, is understated but essential in the everyday practicalities of running a successful team set-up. Often first in and last out of training and matches in preparing kits and equipment, a kit manager fulfils a noble tradition of behind-the-scenes team building.

The contents of Tommy's kit bag are functional and varied. They include footballs, replacement bootlaces, plasters, spare socks and pliers to adjust boot studs. The task of kit manager is not merely cross-checking the contents of the bag but preparing the contents before they even go in it. Tommy has been a constant presence within Kildare football since the mid-1990s. He has been involved in various guises from kitman to caretaker and everything in between. Tommy is very often the first person a player meets when they join the panel.

Longevity is a trait of many GAA kit managers. Colm 'Bandy' McGuigan has been involved with the Derry football team for over twenty-five years, Ollie Walsh has looked after kits for the Laois footballers since the 1980s, and in Tipperary John 'Hotpoint' Hayes departed after giving the hurlers thirty consecutive years of service. In February 2022, Tommy was the recipient of the Gradaim an Uachtaráin, an award which acknowledges his outstanding commitment and long service across the club and county network.

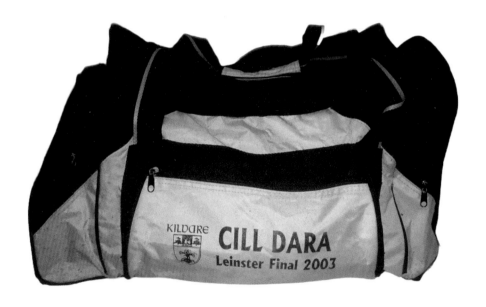

83. Signed Armagh Ladies Football Jersey (2005)

GAA Museum, Croke Park (on loan from Caroline O'Hanlon)

Caroline O'Hanlon has played for the Armagh ladies footballers for over twenty years. This is the jersey that she wore when they captured the junior All-Ireland title by beating Sligo in 2005. A year later, Armagh reached the senior All-Ireland final, which they narrowly lost to Cork. The jersey is signed by Caroline and her teammates; their signatures have transformed the jersey from an object of Caroline's private nostalgia to a material representation of the entirety, of which she was an essential part.

Caroline was nominated for an All-Star award on eleven occasions and won the award three times. In 2006, she was part of the Ireland team in the first ladies International Rules series. She achieved these milestones while playing netball to a high standard in the UK Super League and serving as captain of the Northern Ireland team. The transferable skills from both sports, such as hand–eye coordination, footwork, and running mechanics have undoubtedly played a role in Caroline reaching her athletic potential. She was chosen to be flag bearer for the Northern Ireland team at the opening ceremony of the 2018 Commonwealth Games in Australia.

In 2018, the Armagh Ladies Gaelic Football Association (LGFA) secured a dormant pitch in Killean and are developing their own permanent headquarters on the site, becoming the first county LGFA squad to have their own dedicated facilities. The grounds were formerly used by St Michael's Football Club, which has now disbanded, opening the door to Armagh LGFA undertaking a thirty-five-year lease for the provision of a community centre and sports pavilion with floodlighting. This facility will allow the Armagh ladies footballers to overcome many of the obstacles and inconsistencies that LGFA teams face, such as poor facilities and difficulties in securing pitches for training.

84. Waterford Crystal Chandelier (2005)

Croke Park Stadium, Dublin

This crystal chandelier was designed and created by Billy Canning (Chief Lighting Designer, Waterford Crystal) and was installed in the players' lounge in Croke Park stadium in 2005. The brief was to design a luminaire that reflects the games of the GAA. It consists of thirty-two footballs to represent each county in Ireland and seventy sliotars to represent each minute in a full championship match, all suspended in mid-air as they would be in play. Using LED technology, the crystal balls and sliotars can change colour to the team colours of the winning team being hosted in the players' lounge.

The players' lounge is a private room which allows the players to unwind after a game with their teammates, friends and family. It is not used after every match, but it is tradition after the All-Ireland finals that both teams converge there afterwards to show comradery. The ethos of the players' lounge shows how Gaelic games is not just a competition or a physical activity, but a sport with an important social component where teams can gather amicably in both victory and defeat.

Waterford Crystal has had many strong and tangible links with the GAA including the sponsorship of competitions, trophies, kits and youth development schemes. Most notably, the Waterford Crystal Cup was a pre-season hurling competition, which began in 2006 and involved Munster county teams and third-level colleges. Much like Waterford Crystal's large-scale manufacturing plant in the city, which closed after entering receivership in 2009, the competition ceased in 2016. It was later replaced with the Munster hurling league.

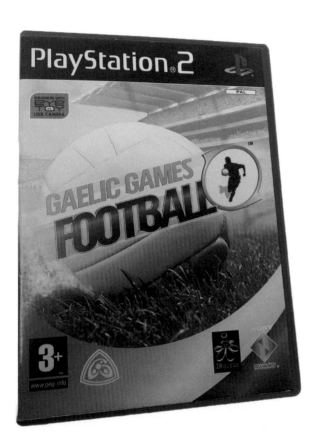

85. *Gaelic Games: Football* PlayStation 2 Game (2005)
Private Collection (Siobhán Doyle, Wexford)

In 1998, the GAA began exploring the idea of bringing Gaelic games to a new dimension as a game on a major computer console. After lengthy negotiations, Australian games development company IR Gurus, who specialise in sports and action games, began its design. This game, *Gaelic Games: Football* was released exclusively for PlayStation 2 in 2005. It was followed by *Gaelic Games: Football 2* and *Gaelic Games: Hurling* in 2007.

The game was launched in Melbourne to coincide with the International Rules series taking place there. It was highly anticipated and reached number one in the Irish PlayStation 2 charts. One eager gamer, Peter Branigan, recalls skipping school (for the first and only time) to purchase *Gaelic Games: Football*. By the end of the day, he had won the league and championship titles with Dublin on the highest difficulty level.

IR Gurus had developed official games for the Australian Football League in 2003, so the GAA equivalent was based on mechanics that were already in place. To allow for greater detail in the players' movements, the game developers used motion capture technology to get the details from Irish players they brought in. The design process faced many challenges including limited resources, time constraints and the design team's lack of familiarity with Gaelic games. The game did not have permission to use official player names and images, so names were randomly generated from the top 100 Irish surnames. Despite sophisticated details on the visuals of venues and jerseys, and with original commentary by Mícheál Ó Muircheartaigh, *Gaelic Games: Football* was criticised for its sluggish performance, lack of speed and intensity, and the ease at which goals could be scored.

86. Tyrone 'GAA 125' Anniversary Jersey (2009)

Cardinal Tomás Ó Fiaich Library, Armagh

On Saturday, 31 January 2009, Tyrone took on Dublin in the opening round of the National Football League as reigning All-Ireland champions. The match marked the beginning of the GAA's 125th anniversary celebrations and was the first in a series of commemorative events around the country throughout that year. This jersey is one of those worn by the Tyrone team during the pre-match warm-up and parade. In keeping with the 'old style' of jersey, it is void of any logos, and features long sleeves, a lace-up collar and a pocket with the red hand of Tyrone and the date printed on it. Dublin also wore specially commissioned jerseys in their colours, which were in a style typical of the 1920s and 1930s rather than of the 1884 event being commemorated.

Two free tickets were allocated to every club in Ireland and the match was played in front of a crowd of over 70,000 spectators in Croke Park, with viewing figures of 210,000 on Setanta Sports. The Dublin team joined a guard of honour to welcome the All-Ireland football champions onto the pitch, alongside minor footballers wearing the jerseys and waving the flags of the thirty-four teams that participate in the All-Ireland championship. Tyrone won on a scoreline of 1–18 to 1–16 on an evening where live entertainment included pageantry, mascots and musical performances from the Artane Senior Band, Sharon Shannon and Mundy. After the game, the floodlights were dimmed and a spectacular pyrotechnics and fireworks display lit up the Dublin skyline.

87. Brian Cody's Cap (*c*.2010s)

Private Collection (Brian Cody, Kilkenny)

The 1999 GAA season was the first of a long and successful managerial career for Brian Cody with the Kilkenny senior hurlers, which lasted until the end of the 2022 intercounty season. Having excelled as a player with his club, James Stephens, and with Kilkenny, claiming All-Ireland medals at minor, under-21 and senior level, Cody transitioned into intercounty management and oversaw Kilkenny's domination of the hurling landscape for many years. Players came and went, records were broken and trophies lifted and returned, but one object that was a mainstay of Cody's management career was his baseball cap. When patrolling the sidelines, Cody's cap, which was swapped for a woolly hat during the winter months, became the most immediately visible part of his attire. Made up of a soft cap and stiff visor, Cody's caps are more functional than fashionable and were just as customary as helmets were to his players.

Historically, hats were a way to impose power and performed an important role in indicating social distinctions. Due to the easing of etiquette, hats fell out of fashion in the second half of the 20th century but there are still unspoken social rules around wearing them, even at GAA matches. It is tradition to remove hats while the national anthem is played and once the hat is removed, it should be held in such a way that only the outside is visible as the inside lining should never be revealed.

Cody's caps were switched regularly in keeping with changes to crests and sponsorship logos. The innovation of printing team crests on caps came in 1902 when the Detroit Tigers baseball team put their namesake on their caps, turning a utilitarian sunshade into a battle flag. The cap's usefulness and brandability became one of America's greatest fashion exports. Hurling's most successful manager embraced the trend and the longevity of the baseball cap as a fashion statement mirrors Cody's longevity as a manager.

88. Flag Trolley (*c*.2010s)

Pearse Park, Longford

Every GAA match that is held, no matter what code or grade, requires preparation beforehand and clean-up afterwards. Tasks such as opening dressing rooms, facilitating crowds and putting goal nets in place are largely undertaken by volunteers, who are an integral part of match-day operations and the organisation as a whole. This trolley is used to carry sideline and goal flags by volunteers in Pearse Park, which is the county grounds of Longford GAA. The trolley is a repurposed hand truck which allows for the easy manoeuvring and storage of the twenty-six flags. On the side of the trolley are official guidelines for the dimensions and markings of pitches for Gaelic football and hurling, as well as the correct placement of each coloured flag.

The purpose of sideline flags is primarily to mark the various crosslines and boundaries of the field because, importantly, a ball that strikes a sideline or corner flag is deemed out of play. They can also be useful in indicating the strength and direction of a blowing breeze, which can often have an effect on the outcome of a game. Sideline flags can vary in colour, with GAA grounds often matching the flag colours to their own club or county colours. In 1966, St Vincent's GAA Club expressed concern to the Cork county board over the height of flags and the danger of players injuring themselves by falling on an upstanding sideline flag, but the matter was not pursued. Guidelines on the size of sideline flags remain vague, but official GAA rules do specify that all flags used on boundary lines must have smooth rounded tops to alleviate the risk of injury. For this reason also, sideline flags, with the exception of the four corner flags, are placed at an angle away from the boundary line.

In 1999, when Waterford won the junior football All-Ireland – the county's first inter-county football title – supporters took to the field in O'Moore Park in Portlaoise after the game and some even took sideline flags home as souvenirs. This forced the grounds-man, Peter Carroll, to source new flags for the ladies' final between Timahoe and Crettyard the following day.

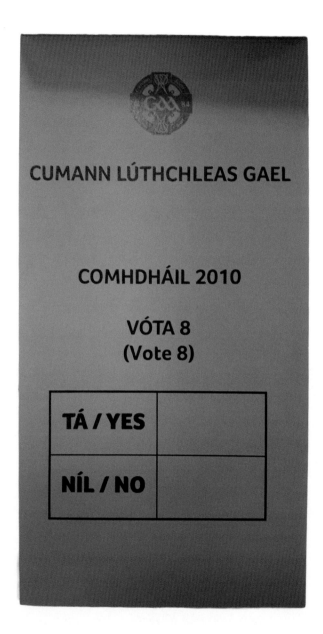

89. GAA Congress Voting Card (2010)

Cardinal Tomás Ó Fiaich Library, Armagh

The GAA Congress is an annual meeting where motions calling for policy or rule changes are debated and voted upon by delegates representing all provinces, counties and other administrative units to determine whether the proposals are entered into the Official Guide of the association. Getting a motion as far as Congress is a complex process which involves it being proposed and passing through sub-committees before being put forward to a vote. This is a voting card from the 2010 Congress, which was distributed to each delegate to allow for their votes to be cast. The voting system has since moved to a more efficient electronic voting system, allowing for results to be viewed on screen immediately afterwards.

The event moves to different locations around the country on an annual basis, and the 2010 Congress was held in Slieve Donard Hotel, Newcastle, Co. Down. At this Congress, 123 motions were debated. Significant changes included the Gaelic Players Association being officially recognised as the representative body for GAA players, and the ban on championship competitions for children up to the age of twelve; these were replaced with a Go Games format which is organised on a blitz basis.

The GAA Congress has been responsible for many landmark changes in the association, including a motion in 2005 that voted to temporarily set aside Rule 42, which prevented sports other than Gaelic games from being played at GAA venues. This allowed the Ireland rugby team and the Republic of Ireland soccer team to play games at Croke Park while Lansdowne Road stadium was being redeveloped. However, the GAA Congress can also be a frustrating affair and has been the scene of many controversial decisions, including that in 1938 to suspend the President of Ireland, Douglas Hyde (1860–1949), from the association due to his attendance at a soccer match. This was in breach of GAA Rule 27, which prevented members of the GAA from playing or attending banned sports. The rule, also known as 'The Ban', was rescinded at GAA Congress in 1971.

90. Hawk-Eye Camera (2011)

© Brian Lawless/Sportsfile

Human mistakes are a facet of Gaelic games, sport and everyday life, yet referees, linesmen and umpires find themselves under intense scrutiny due to their interpretation of the rules of play and judgement calls. To preserve the legitimacy of decision-making and to assist officials when awarding points, the GAA introduced technology known as Hawk-Eye. This is one of eight high-speed cameras located in Croke Park that generates a 3D image and can then rule whether or not a ball has gone between the posts and fully over the crossbar or not. The innovative points detection system is operated by an official based in the stadium's event control room who communicates with the referee via an audio signal within seconds of the sliotar crossing the line. Hawk-Eye provides real-time imagery on the stadium's big screen of the ball's trajectory over the posts to remove any ambiguity over whether a point was scored or missed.

At the GAA Congress in 2013, 86 per cent of delegates voted in favour of the introduction of Hawk-Eye. The technology was first used in Croke Park later that year before it was extended to Semple Stadium in Thurles in 2016. Hawk-Eye does not intervene in every decision or even in every match played in these stadiums. The technology is implemented only when deemed necessary by the umpires or referee, or when the umpires have incorrectly awarded a point. A momentous call was made by Hawk-Eye at the end of the 2014 All-Ireland senior hurling final between Tipperary and Kilkenny. With the scores level, John 'Bubbles' O'Dwyer of Tipperary hit a last-gasp free, which thousands of supporters believed to be the winning point. However, Hawk-Eye ruled that the ball went wide and sent the match to a replay two weeks later, which Kilkenny won.

Hawk-Eye made headlines again in 2022 when a hardware failure resulted in the system denying Galway's Shane Walsh a point during the first half of the All-Ireland football semi-final versus Derry. The decision was reversed at half-time after replays indicated that his shot had clearly gone between the posts. Galway went on to win the game by 2–8 to 1–6.

91. Rubber Bas Hurl (2018)

Private Collection (Pat Carty, Tourlestrane)

The GAA is committed to inclusion and diversity at all levels, and with this in mind, an official GAA sport for people with disabilities was developed. Wheelchair hurling was created in 1998 by Tim Maher, originally from Lixnaw, Co. Kerry. As a teacher in a residential school for children with physical disabilities attached to St Mary's Hospital in Baldoyle, Co. Dublin, the potential for wheelchair hurling occurred to Tim when watching his students playing tennis. He sourced a set of 24-inch hurls and his idea spread to other schools in Dublin. A league began and in 2011 the first All-Ireland wheelchair tournament took place. This is the hurl used by Pat Carty from Tourlestrane, Co. Sligo, captain of the Irish wheelchair hurling team.

Some disability sports are adapted sports – traditional sports slightly modified to meet the needs of people with a disability, and as such, the equipment requires adapting as well. This hurl, created by Cultec, has a modified rubber end (or bas) that is suited to the indoor environment where wheelchair hurling is played. The preferred playing area is a full-size basketball court, which is split into three zones: attacking half, defensive half and goalkeeper's area. Wheelchair hurling teams are six-a-side and the total playing time of a match is thirty minutes. Aside from goalkeepers being allowed to use their hands to catch a ball and hand-pass it off, the game is primarily ground hurling and goals are worth three points, while a point can only be scored from a sideline cut.

The M. Donnelly GAA interprovincial wheelchair hurling tournament now takes place annually, with thirty wheelchair athletes from all four provinces participating. The hope is to increase participation and optimise playing standards to support this important expansion in Gaelic games.

92. Fundraising Wall (2019)

Leitrim GAA Centre of Excellence, Annaduff

Finance is a fundamental aspect of the modern GAA and fundraising is an essential part of any club and county set-up. Though financial assistance is given through the Central Council, provincial councils and philanthropy, innovation is necessary in order to entice contributions from the public. In 2018, Leitrim GAA launched the 'Leitrim Wall Campaign' to fund their state-of-the-art facility for training all county football, hurling and handball teams.

A land purchase deal was completed in 2005 in Annaduff for the development of the county's Centre of Excellence. After this, a fundraising committee was put in place and came up with the campaign where Leitrim supporters could buy a brick in one of five specially built walls located at the centre's entrance. There are four options of four different designs, sizes and prices. Each brick records a personalised message, with many using the brick to commemorate a deceased loved one and their love for Leitrim. Many bricks were purchased by the Leitrim diaspora, highlighting the great bond of family and community in a county with so many emigrants.

The scheme was launched in Rory Dolan's bar in Yonkers on the eve of Leitrim's Connacht championship clash with New York in May 2018 – a fixture which usually marks the beginning of the championship season. Leitrim senior footballer's success in the 2019 league brought a level of excitement and hope for the county not seen since their provincial win in 1994, and with it came a rush to buy the bricks. The scheme is an example of collective identity on public display and provides something tangible and permanent for people to express their support for the county.

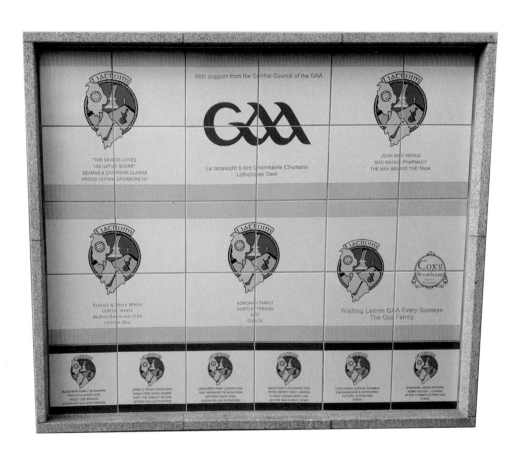

93. Artane Band Tunic (2019)

Artane School of Music

In 1871, the Artane Band was formed when Brother Thomas Alphonsus Hoope brought together a band of young musicians from the boys' school that was soon to be officially established in Artane, Co. Dublin. In the GAA's infancy, the association approached the band to play at a match and so began a unique and long-standing relationship that exists to the present day. Like a team wearing their traditional team colours, the Artane Band expresses its identity through its uniform of distinct blue and red.

This tunic is part of the full uniform which comprises tunic, trousers, cap and black shoes. The uniform has changed over time, with heavy wool fabrics being replaced with cotton and polyester blends for added comfort and movement. The seven gold buttons that run down the centre of the tunic are emblazoned with an image of a music stand that features in the Artane Band's logo. The uniform has become iconic and is synonymous with big match days in Croke Park. However, in 1969 the band was forced to perform during the Railway Cup finals without their traditional uniforms, which were lost in a fire at the school.

A major change came about in 2004, when, for the first time in its history, membership of the band was opened to girls and the word 'Boys' was officially dropped from the name of the band. To date, the band has played for every President and Taoiseach of Ireland, as well as many heads of state and famous figures. They play a blend of old and new songs, with 'God Save Ireland' being a constant on the setlist as the forty band members lead the team parade around the field.

94. Five-in-a-row Manhole Cover (2019)

Grand Canal Dock, Dublin

In 2019, the Dublin footballers made history by becoming the first team to lift the Sam Maguire Cup for five consecutive years. Dublin City Council marked this achievement in GAA history by commissioning specially designed manhole covers around the city. They were created by Oonagh Young, designer and director of Design HQ – a graphic design communications company based in Dublin city. The concept for the commemorative manhole covers was an initiative of Dublin City Council in consultation with Dublin GAA. There are twenty-seven covers which are located around Grand Canal Plaza, George's Dock and continue to Mayor Street on the capital's northside.

Manhole covers serve as an access point for subsurface utilities, but they are also an intrinsic part of the patchwork of villages, towns and cities. They act as markers for streets and can often tell us about the history of a place. The unique design cast into the surface is functional as it adds grip to the metal covers and prevents them becoming dangerous in wet conditions. It incorporates the Dublin GAA crest, which has been in use since 2004. The crest envisions Dublin's historical past and its geographical spread: the castle in flames representing the city (this is also on the Dublin city crest); the raven signifying the county of Fingal; the book of St Tamlacht (Tallaght) representing south Dublin; and the Viking longboat signifying Dún Laoghaire-Rathdown.

The manhole covers demonstrate how even the most mundane, unremarkable objects can become artworks as well as instruments of commemoration. In December 2020, Dublin went on to win a record sixth senior title in a row and in September 2021, the Dublin ladies footballers chased another five-in-a-row for the county. They were eventually beaten in the final by Meath, who captured their first ever All-Ireland ladies senior title.

95. *Transilience* (2020) by David Sweeney

GAA Museum, Croke Park

Centenaries mark the passing of 100 years; with history gone beyond living memory, they are opportunities for the creation of new interpretations of people, places and events. This painting was specially commissioned by the GAA Museum in anticipation of the centenary of Bloody Sunday and was the visual centrepiece of the GAA's commemorations in 2020. The title *Transilience* means an abrupt change or leaping from one state to another, which reflects the events that unfolded in Croke Park on 21 November 1920. British soldiers opened fire during a football match there, killing fourteen people in one of the most significant atrocities of the War of Independence.

The painting is oils on board and took three months to complete. It is by artist David Sweeney, a former Dublin GAA senior hurling captain who took up painting when he stepped away from intercounty hurling. His objective in creating this artwork was to invoke the memory of Bloody Sunday and also to incorporate the community and locality around Croke Park. The scene is of Russell Street, which runs towards what is now known as the Hogan Stand, named after Michael Hogan, one of the victims of Bloody Sunday.

The portrayal of a colourful, contemporary match-day streetscape with Dublin and Tipperary supporters is torn down the middle of the canvas with a monochrome depiction of an armoured vehicle carrying Black and Tans towards Croke Park. Overhead, an aeroplane trails a flare which signalled to the British forces to move in on the stadium. The match-day supporters are unaware of this looming presence on the canvas, just like those in Croke Park on that fateful day.

96. Cúl Camp Backpack (2021)

Private Collection (Jessica Doyle, Wexford)

GAA summer camps were first organised on an ad hoc basis in the 1980s and were aimed largely at primary schoolchildren to help them learn and develop sport and life skills by participating in Gaelic games. The growth in numbers attending the camps established a need for their organisation on a national basis and from this, GAA Cúl Camps was formalised in 2006 in a streamlined manner. This ensured a standardisation of quality and principles nationwide, with the camps' success reflecting the continuing development of GAA coaching.

Since 2006, over one million children aged six to thirteen have participated in Cúl Camps, which run for one week in the summer months. The activities take a games-based approach which revolves around enjoyment and sustaining participation in Gaelic games. Each child participating in Cúl Camps receives a jersey, zip top and a backpack. Generally, the gear does not go on public sale and as such is a manifestation of being part of an exclusive collective of those participating in Cúl Camps. Embedded with logos and with a different design on an annual basis, Cúl Camps gear is a uniform that encourages the wearer to feel comfortable, confident and ready to play GAA. The backpacks in particular are convenient for transporting match-day essentials, such as the traditional flasks, sandwiches and snacks.

Cúl Camps continue to be one of the most popular community recreation settings for children during the summer holidays. In 2019, Wexford GAA developed the first specialised Cúl Camp for autistic children, which involved creating a more sensory friendly experience for attendees and their siblings, who also participated. This initiative has paved the way for more of its kind across the country, and encompasses the spirit of community and inclusion of children with different abilities across the GAA.

97. All-Ireland Final Yellow Sliotar (2020)

Private Collection (Pa Buckley, Limerick)

The 2020 hurling season saw many unavoidable changes to fixtures, attendances and match-day procedures due to the Covid-19 pandemic. One notable change that was external to health regulations was the introduction of the yellow sliotar as the standard colour for intercounty matches. The luminous ball allows for increased visibility at a distance and when passing in front of floodlights, clouds, goalposts and sidelines. This yellow sliotar was used in the All-Ireland hurling final between Limerick and Waterford – the first final to be played behind closed doors without supporters.

A major problem identified with the traditional white sliotar is that it does not contrast sufficiently with backgrounds such as sky and surroundings, which is not only a difficulty for supporters but crucially for players and officials. As part of the process to improve the sliotar, the GAA's games development committee was advised by optometrists and other specialists in the design process. To improve the visibility of the sliotar further, a shade of yellow referred to as florescent or 'optic' yellow was adopted.

The change of colour is a similar approach that tennis took in 1972, making the ball more visible for television, which had moved from monochrome to colour coverage. In 2021, the yellow sliotar became the standard colour for intercounty matches, but there have been varied responses from players, spectators and television viewers, many of whom believe the change in colour is unnecessary. The discussion over the most suitable weight of a sliotar is also ongoing, demonstrating how an ideal form of sliotar that is widely accepted may be elusive. Nevertheless, the sliotar does not have a passive presence in hurling and its design must be continuously improved so that it can move along with advancements in technology and research.

98. Gaeil Ruairí Óg Mural (2021)

Ruáirí Óg GAA, Cushendall

When art is placed in a public setting for daily passers-by, it becomes a means for communicating a certain message to a large audience. Murals are large-scale artworks designed for this purpose and they have a significant presence across the north of Ireland in particular. Within a GAA context, the village of Cushendall, Co. Antrim, has a strong tradition of community murals. Featuring the local GAA team, legendary players and famous club members, murals are not only displayed in the village, but they have become part of the scenery of the village itself. Gaeil Ruairí Óg, the language and cultural department of Ruairí Óg GAA Club, created a mural that shifted the aim from simply creating a work of art, to incorporating the children of the community in the mural-making process.

Artist Fiona McAuley guided forty-eight children to create a large-scale mural project that would allow them to represent the club through art. The mural depicts 16th-century rebel Ruairí Óg Ó Mórdha dressed in a traditional cape and sandals surrounded by children playing hurling and camogie. The maroon and white club colours are central throughout, with a border along the bottom featuring vibrant Celtic knots. The mural contains symbols of the local area including Lurigethan Mountain and the Atlantic Ocean, as well as the slogan 'Ní neart go cur le chéile' (there's no strength without unity). The mural is located in the clubhouse, which is a community space designed not only to facilitate GAA teams, but for people to interact socially. The mural was created during the Covid-19 pandemic in March 2021 and is an important message of unity during a challenging time.

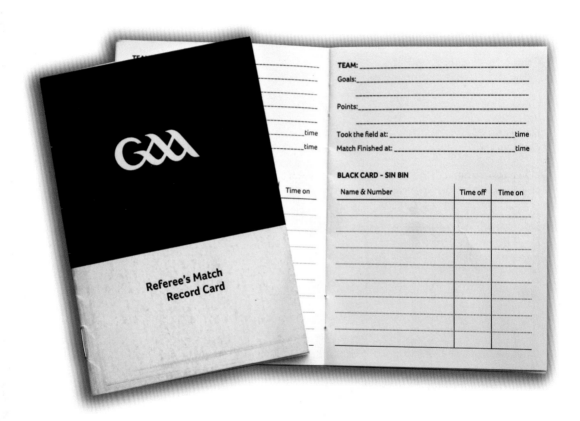

TEAM: _____

TEAM: _____
Goals: _____
_____
Points: _____
_____

Took the field at: _____ time
Match Finished at: _____ time

_____ time
_____ time

BLACK CARD – SIN BIN

Name & Number	Time off	Time on

Time on

GAA

Referee's Match
Record Card

99. Maggie Farrelly's Referee Report Card (2021)
Private Collection (Maggie Farrelly, Co. Cavan)

A referee's report card is an important part of their kit as it allows for the recording of teams, officials, times, scores, substitutions, injuries and details of players cautioned. It is contained in the referee's wallet and is used to complete the referee's report after each match. This match record card belongs to Maggie Farrelly, who has achieved a series of firsts as a female referee. In 2015, Maggie was the first woman to referee a men's intercounty Gaelic football match when Fermanagh played Antrim in the Ulster minor championship. She followed this by officiating her first senior men's intercounty game in the McKenna Cup in 2016 and the Cavan senior football final replay in November 2021, and with her addition to the national panel of referees in 2022.

Refereeing has historically been a role targeted exclusively at men, but Maggie follows in the footsteps of a scarce cohort of female referees in men's codes. Marie Curtis refereed underage games in Laois in 1989, having qualified as a referee in March 1988. Mary Gannon was an umpire in a Meath junior football championship match between Dunboyne and Baconstown in 1980, while her husband Joe refereed the same game. In 1990, Edel Clarke was appointed as a men's referee in Westmeath. Although there is still much work to be done in creating a more gender-balanced association, the GAA has revised its restrictions in order to be more inclusive. Maggie's officiating in high-profile matches encourages acceptance of women in visible and authoritative roles in the association, and highlights that Gaelic games – and indeed more widely, sport in general – is for all individuals, genders and identities.

100. Sculpture of Richard 'Droog' Walsh by Seamus Connolly (2021)

© Joe Cashin, Mooncoin

Statues in public spaces offer a particular insight into the cultural landscape, often helping to collect, embody and communicate public memory and collective identity. This is the statue of Richard 'Droog' Walsh (1877–1958) from the studio of sculptor Seamus Connolly in Co. Clare. The hurl in the sculpture was based on one that was owned by Richard and found in a family home in recent years. In October 2021, the finished life-size sculpture was unveiled on Main Street, Mooncoin, Co. Kilkenny, where Richard grew up.

Richard was the first player to captain a hurling team to three All-Ireland titles when Kilkenny won in 1907, 1909 and 1913. The 1913 match was the first fifteen-a-side final and also the first final in which Kilkenny wore their famous black-and-amber vertical stripes, which became the official Kilkenny colours. Richard was affectionately known as Dick or 'Droog', owing to his party piece being a rendition of the historical folk song 'The Bold Dragoon'.

Statues dedicated to individuals associated with the GAA have become more widespread in the last ten years. These are usually free-standing and erected in the community where the individuals came from, often in the sanctuary where their games took place. Seamus Connolly has been the sculptor of many of these statues including those memorialising Dermot Earley (Gortaganny, Co. Roscommon), Mick Mackey (Castleconnell, Co. Limerick), Gerry O'Malley (Bridewell, Co. Roscommon) and Páidí Ó Sé (Ventry, Co. Kerry).

Bibliography

Introduction

Cnoc na Gaoithe online, accessed 12 January 2022.

Day, Dave & Wray Vamplew, 'Sports History Methodology: Old and New', *The International Journal of the History of Sport* 32(15): 1715–24 (2015).

The Freeman's Journal, 23 September 1880, p. 30.

Irish Independent, 10 April 1956, p. 10.

Kilkenny People, 22 January 1965, p. 6.

Kilkenny People, 1 June 1979, p. 14.

Littleton, Joe, Cloney Quin GAA online, 'The Carrahan Flag – A Beauty to Behold', accessed 4 November 2021.

MacGregor, Neil, *A History of the World in 100 Objects* (London: Penguin, 2012).

Morris, Rachel, *The Museum Makers: A Journey Backwards – from Old Boxes of Dark Family Secrets to a Golden Era of Museums* (Tewkesbury: September Publishing, 2020).

Munster Express, 15 March 1957, p. 13.

Munster Express, 10 July 1953, p. 9.

Munster Express, 10 January 1958, p. 10.

Munster Express, 25 October 1968, p. 9.

Nenagh Guardian, 7 September 1957, p. 5.

O'Toole, Fintan, *A History of Ireland in 100 Objects* (Royal Irish Academy: Dublin, 2013).

Pope, S.W. and John Nauright, 'Introduction' in *Routledge Companion to Sports History*, edited by S. W. Pope and John Nauright (London/New York: Routledge, 2009), pp. 3–11.

Stearns, Peter N, 'Foreword' in *Routledge Companion to Sports History*, edited by S.W. Pope and John Nauright (London/New York: Routledge, 2009), pp. x–xv.

Waterford News and Star, 19 December 1961, p. 3.

100 GAA Objects

1. Wooden Mether

Earwood, Caroline, 'Bog Butter: A Two Thousand Year History', *The Journal of Irish Archaeology* 8: 25–42 (1997).

Croke Park online, 'Liam MacCarthy Cup: Corn Mhic Cárthaigh', accessed 15 November 2021.

The Cork Examiner, 21 May 1929, p. 7.

National Museum of Ireland online, 'Medieval Irish Mether', accessed 17 August 2021.

Ó Ceallachain, Sean Óg, *Evening Press*, 22 January 1979, p. 11.

O'Sullivan, Catherine Marie, *Hospitality in Medieval Ireland, 900–1500* (Dublin: Four Courts Press, 2004).

2. Hair Hurling Ball

Doyle, Clodagh, 'Hair Hurling Balls: Review, Research and Scientific Investigations', *Folk Life* 54(1): 3–31 (2016).

Doyle, Clodagh, National Museum of Ireland online, 'May Day', 24 July 2021.

Wertmann, Patrick, Xinyong Chen, Xiao Li, Dongliang Xu, Pavel E. Tarasov and Mayke Wagner, 'New evidence for ball games in Eurasia from ca. 3000-year-old Yanghai tombs in the Turfan depression of Northwest China', *Journal of Archaeological Science* 34, Part B (2020).

O'Sullivan, P.M., 'Hair balls combed from hurling's ancient history', *Irish Examiner* online, published 24 August 2017.

3. Illustration of Handball Game

Chris Beetles Gallery online, 'John Nixon (before 1759–1818)', accessed 5 November 2021.

Department of Arts, Heritage and the Gaeltacht, *An Introduction to the Architectural Heritage of County Monaghan* (Dublin: Government of Ireland, 2013).

GAA Handball online, 'History', accessed 15 December 2021.

NUI Galway online, 'A Ban on Ye Small Ball', published 4 October 2012.

4. 'Citie of the Tribes' Banner

City Tribune, 7 December 2001, p. 4.

GAA.ie, 'Gaelic Sunday', accessed 28 January 2022.

Galway City Museum online, 'The Tribes of Galway', accessed 20 January 2022.

Galway GAA online, 'Galway Senior Hurling Club Finals 1887–2020', accessed 28 January 2022.

The Irish Press, 12 April 1984, p. 9.

Rouse, Paul, 'What's the real story of Gaelic Sunday?', *Irish Examiner* online, published 3 August 2018.

5. Michael Cusack's Blackthorn Stick

Andersson, Peter K., 'The walking stick in the nineteenth-century city: Conflicting ideals of urban walking', *Journal of Transport History* 39(3): 275–91 (2018).

Foley, Cliona, *Evening Herald*, 20 June 1997, p. 89.

Hurley, John W., *Shillelagh: The Irish Fighting Stick* (Pipersville, PA: Caravat Press, 2011).

Kavanagh, Peter, 'A Weapon of Honor: The Shillelagh', *The American Mercury*: 525–31 (May 1951).

Quinn, James, 'Cusack, Michael', Dictionary of Irish Biography online.

Reid, Philip, *Evening Press*, 17 May 1984, p. 11.

6. Letter from Michael Cusack to Maurice Davin

National Library of Ireland online, 'Michael Cusack, Maurice Davin and the Gaelic Athletic Association', accessed 31 October 2021.

7. Bray Emmets Banner

Croke Park online, 'A treasure trove of GAA and Irish History', 29 September 2021.

The Freeman's Journal, 21 November 1892, p. 2.

The Freeman's Journal, 28 March 1884, p. 1.

Irish Independent, 5 September 1970, p. 1.

Whelan, Kevin, 'Robert Emmet: Between History and Memory', *History Ireland* online, accessed 2 October 2021.

8. Davitt and Croke Commemorative Plate

Harrington, John, GAA.ie, 'Michael Davitt Remembered', published 25 March 2020.

Kirby, Brian, 'Leaving Certificate History Case Study: The GAA to 1891', National Library of Ireland online, accessed 18 August 2021.

Trinity College Dublin online, 'Michael Davitt and the Gaelic Athletic Association', published 11 February 2021.

9. GAA Rule Book

GAA.ie, 'Gaelic Athletic Association (established 1884) Official Guide – Part 1', accessed 16 November 2021.

Kilkenny People, 29 March 1913, p. 5.

Nic Congáil, Ríona, 'Young Ireland and The Nation: Nationalist Children's Culture in the Late Nineteenth Century', *Éire-Ireland* 46 (3&4): 37–62 (Fall/Winter 2011).

10. Handball signed by Fr Tom Jones

Austin Stacks GAA online, 'Fr Tom Jones 1868–1950', published 19 December 2018.

Clarke, J.K., 'Father Tom Jones of Kerry', *Journal of the Layman's Association of Maynooth College*, Vexilla Regis: 76 (1965).

Fitzgerald, Eamonn, 'The Days of Handball in Killarney', Spa GAA online, accessed 9 October 2021.

Francis, Tom, *Holly Bough*, 25 December 1982, p. 23.

Kerry Press, 4 August 1914, p. 4.

The Kerryman North Edition, 3 February 2005, Section: Tralee.

O'Gorman, Jude, 'Fr. Tom Jones – Handball Player and Hero', *The Kerry Magazine* 23: 43–4 (2013).

Rouse, John, 'Jones, Thomas (Tom)', Dictionary of Irish Biography.

11. Tubberdora Cap

Lár na Páirce online, 'Treasures of Lár na Páirce: 2. Tubberdora Cap', 27 January 2022.

Meath Chronicle, 16 March 1996, p. 28.

Rouse, Paul, *The Hurlers: The First All-Ireland Championship and the Making of Modern Hurling* (Dublin: Penguin, 2018).

12. Aghabullogue Hurl

Irish Independent, 4 December 1974, p. 17.

The Irish Press, 17 February 1965, p. 16.

The Kerryman, 10 December 1938, p. 28.

Kilmurry Museum online, 'Aghabullogue Hurley – Cork's First All Ireland Title', accessed 2 June 2022.

The Southern Star, 11 September 1954, p. 6.

13. All-Ireland Football Challenge Cup

Evening Herald, 16 March 1901, p. 7.

Kelleher, Humphrey, *GAA Family Silver: The People and Stories Behind 101 Cups and Trophies* (Dublin: Sportsfile, 2013).

14. Archbishop Croke Stained-glass Window

National Inventory of Architectural Heritage online, 'Cathedral of the Assumption, Cathedral Street, Thurles Townparks, Thurles, Tipperary North', accessed 11 July 2021.

Thurles Parish, 'Our Story/History', accessed 11 July 2021.

Tierney, Mark, *Croke of Cashel: The Life of Archbishop Thomas William Croke 1832–1902* (Dublin: Gill & Macmillan, 1976).

Woods, C.J., 'Croke, Thomas William', Dictionary of Irish Biography, published October 2009.

15. Illustration of Gaelic Footballer by George Fagan

Breathnach, Teresa, 'Greeting the Nation – The Irish Christmas Card', *History Ireland* online, accessed 28 October 2021.

Buildings of Ireland online, 'Sony Centre/Indulge, 16–17 O'Connell Street Lower, Sackville Place, Dublin 1, DUBLIN', accessed 15 August 2021.

RTÉ.ie, 'Doc on One: The All-Ireland Behind Barbed Wire', published 15 April 2016.

16. Map of Croke Park

Carey, Tim, *Croke Park: A History* (Cork: Collins Press, 2005).

Duffy, Páraic and Gearóid Ó Tuathaigh, 'Croke Park' in *GAA and Revolution in Ireland 1913–1923*, edited by Gearóid Ó Tuathaigh (Cork: Collins Press, 2016), pp. 37–52.

Education Department, GAA Museum, *The Gaelic Athletic Association Through History and Documents 1870–1920* (Dublin: GAA Museum, 2008).

O'Grady, Gerrard, *Tipperary Star*, 1 September 1984, p. 31.

Rouse, Paul, 'Dineen, Frank Brazil', Dictionary of Irish Biography, published October 2009.

17. Dublin County Board Minutes

GAA.ie, 'Pride in the (changed) Jersey', published 29 May 2010.

The Irish Press, 13 October 1965, p. 15.

O'Duinn, Tomas, 'An Irishman's Diary', *The Irish Times*, 16 May 2000.

18. Dick Fitzgerald's Coaching Manual

East Kerry GAA online, 'Celebration Centenary Publication Dick Fitzgerald Book', 3 August 2021.

Fitzgerald, Dick, *How to Play Gaelic Football* (Cork: Guy & Co, 1914).

McGuire, Andrew and Hassan, David, 'Dick Fitzgerald – A Revolutionary Like No Other', *Sport in History* 33(4): 532–53 (2013).

19. Silver Mounted Camán

Highlife Highland online, 'Blogpost #3 – Shinty Through the Wars', accessed 12 October 2021.

Highlife Highland online, 'Blogpost #4 – The Camanachd Cup', accessed 12 October 2021.

Shinty online, 'History', accessed 12 October 2021.

Whelan, Kevin, 'The Geography of Hurling', *History Ireland* online, accessed 8 October 2021.

20. Letter from Bob O'Keeffe to John J. Higgins

The Irish Times online, '"New" cup comes with a history', published 29 June 2005.

Laois GAA online, 'Bailiúchán John J. Higgins, Leix and Ossory GAA, 1914–1917', accessed 19 December 2021.

Rouse, Paul, 'How Leix won the All-Ireland Hurling Championship of 1915', RTÉ.ie, accessed 19 December 2021.

21. GAA of USA Medal

Cullen, Emily, 'Summoning Her Children to Which Flag?', *History Ireland* online, published 2016.

GAA.ie, '1915 GAA of USA Medal', accessed 3 April 2022.

GAA.ie, 'New York', accessed 3 April 2022.

Harrington, John, 'New York GAA developing a generation of homegrown heroes', GAA.ie, published 21 April 2021.

Kilkenny People, 21 August 1909, p. 9.

RTÉ.ie, 'The rise and rise of camogie in the Big Apple', published 25 November 2019.

'Charlestown', *Western People*, 9 December 1998, p. 69.

22. Poster Banning GAA Events

Duncan, Mark, 'The West Awakes: The story of Mayo footballers & the 1916 All-Ireland final', RTÉ.ie, accessed 26 October 2021.

Independent.ie, 'The GAA and the Rising', accessed 26 October 2021.

Smyth, William J., 'Conflict, Reaction and Control in Nineteenth-Century Ireland: The Archaeology of Revolution' in *Atlas of the Irish Revolution*, edited by John Crowley, Donal Ó Drisceoil, Mike Murphy and John Borgonovo (Cork: Cork University Press, 2017), pp. 21–55.

23. Rounders Bat

Kilmainham Graffiti online, 23 July 2021.

Maume, Patrick, 'Humphreys, Sighle (Mary Ellen; Sighle Bean Uí Dhonnchadha)', Dictionary of Irish Biography, published October 2009.

24. Bootlace from Bloody Sunday

Croke Park online, 'Key Artefacts from Bloody Sunday', accessed 14 July 2021.

Foley, Michael, 'Remembering Michael Hogan', GAA.ie, published 4 November 2020.

Foley, Michael, *The Bloodied Field: Croke Park. Sunday 21 November 1920* (Dublin: O'Brien Press, 2020).

Tipperary Star, 10 August 1999, p. 10.

25. Sideline Flag from Ballykinlar Internment Camp

Belfast Telegraph online, 'Ballykinler Army Base to Become GAA Centre', published 5 August 2017.

GAA.ie, 'Planning approved for Down GAA Centre at Ballykinlar', published 28 July 2021.

Kilmainham Gaol Archives, KMGLM.19NW-1D23-28, *The Barbed Wire* 1 (1) (Ballykinlar Camps 2: August 1921).

National Museum of Ireland online, 'Internment, Imprisonment and Escape', accessed 16 September 2021.

26. Haughney Memorial Cup

Carlow IGP online, 'Denis "Buller" Haughney', accessed 19 February 2022.

The Nationalist and Leinster Times, 21 October 1922, p. 5.

The Nationalist and Leinster Times, 7 June 1924, p. 5.

The Nationalist online, 'The Nationalist Sponsors New Cup for Carlow Football Championship', published 13 October 2017.

27. Sam Maguire's Pocket Watch

Burton, Gregory, 'The History of the Pocket Watch', Frankenmuth Clock online, accessed 16 February 2022.

Cronin, Mike, 'Sam Maguire: Forgotten Hero and National Icon', *Sport in History* 25(2): 189–205 (2005).

GAA.ie, 'Sam Maguire Pocket Watch', accessed 17 February 2022.

Thompson, Clive, 'The Pocket Watch Was the World's First Wearable Tech Game Changer', *Smithsonian Magazine* online, published June 2014.

28. Gold Medal from Tailteann Games

Australia Olympics online, 'Ivan Stedman', accessed 26 July 2021.

Caufield RSL online, 'Ivan Stedman', accessed 26 July 2021.

Independent.ie, 'Flashback: Ireland's answer to the Olympic Games', published 22 August 2016.

Rouse, Paul, 'When Ireland's Tailteann Games eclipsed the Olympics', *Irish Examiner* online, published 18 November 2016.

Rouse, Paul, *Sport in Ireland: A History* (Oxford, Oxford University Press, 2015).

29. Diary of US Tour

Duncan, Mark, 'Looking back on the Tipperary hurlers 1926 US tour', *The Irish Times* online, published 2 September 2016.

Nenagh Guardian, 26 June 1926, p. 1.

Nenagh Guardian, 15 September 1928, p. 7.

Lár na Páirce online, 'Treasure No 33 – Historic Manuscript of 1926 Tipperary Tour of the US', accessed 2 January 2022.

30. Account Book from Gaelic Field, Dungarvan

Irish Examiner, 25 October 1984, p. 16.

Limerick Leader, 26 January 1974, p. 35.

'Major Role', *The Southern Star*, 9 March 1974, p. 14.

The National Archives of Ireland online, 'Sport and Culture in Waterford in the early 20th century', accessed 16 August 2021.

Waterford County Museum online, 'Biography – Fraher, Dan', accessed 16 August 2021.

31. *The Tipperary Hurler* by Seán Keating

Dublin City Gallery, 'Keating Seán', The Hugh Lane online, accessed 14 July 2021.

O'Connor, Éimear, *Seán Keating Art, Politics and Building the Irish Nation* (Dublin: Irish Academic Press, 2013).

Parsons, Michael, 'Art mystery solved as Keating portrait goes on display at Hugh Lane Gallery', *The Irish Times* online, published 22 August 2009.

Rouse, Paul, 'Keating portrait truly a picture that paints a thousand words', *Irish Examiner* online, published 26 October 2018.

Thurles Information online, 'The Tipperary Hurler', accessed 14 July 2021.

32. John Joe Doyle's Protective Goggles

Burke, Ray, *The Irish Press*, 7 September 1987, p. 1.

Fallon, John, *City Tribune*, 11 August 1995, p. 18.

Woods, Con, 'The Famous Goggles', Cora Chaitlin CLG online, accessed 13 July 2021.

33. Henry Kenny's Leather Boots

Flanagan, Ger, 'His Contribution Has Been Immense', *Mayo News* online, 14 May 2019.

Mac Dubhghaill, Uinsionn, 'County of a certain stripe gears up to lift the cup', *The Irish Times* online, 12 September 1996.

McMorrow, Conor, *Dáil Stars: From Croke Park to Leinster House* (Dublin: Mentor Books, 2010).

34. Hurleymaker's Spokeshave

Irish Independent, 16 July 1934, p. 7.

O'Donoghue, Anne, 'Podcast: From ash to bamboo with Torpey Hurleys', *Farmer's Journal* online, 12 May 2021.

Sweeney, Peter, 'Ash dieback and the fine art of hurley making', GAA.ie, 3 May 2016.

The Historic Dockyard Chatham online, 'Spokeshave', accessed 14 December 2021.

YouTube, Tanera Camans, 'Hurl Making (From Ash to Clash)', uploaded 22 October 2016.

35. Fermanagh Exiles Team Sash

The Anglo-Celt, 14 March 1996, p. 4.

Fermanagh Herald, 2 September 1998, p. 33.

Fermanagh Herald, 27 June 1964, p. 11.

Fermanagh Herald, 16 June 1934, p. 9.

Fermanagh Herald, 12 April 1930, p. 5.

Getty Thesaurus online, 'Sashes', accessed 13 October 2021.

36. South Africa Flag from Tailteann Games

The Freeman's Journal, 28 June 1923, p. 6.

The Freeman's Journal, 1 August 1924, p. 7.

Limerick Leader, 30 April 1932, p. 1.

37. Gold Pin from Camogie Tournament

All of the Ball online, 'O'Duffy comes to Leeside – Cork Camogie's first title', accessed 28 September 2021.

Carter, Plunkett, 'The definite history of the Ban and Cork GAA, 50 years on from Rule 27 ending', Echo Live online, published 11 April 2021.

Fox, Maureen, *Irish Examiner*, 30 August 1996, p. 66.

The Irish Press, 27 December 1933, p. 10.

The Southern Star, 23 September 1933, p. 11.

The Camogie Association online, 'History', accessed 14 December 2021.

38. GAA Golden Jubilee Postage Stamp

Cannon, Joseph, *Irish Independent*, 25 September 1946, p. 4.

Evening Echo, 23 February 1935, p. 8.

Irish Examiner, 26 March 1934, p. 5.

The Irish Press, 17 July 1934, p. 7.

The Irish Press, 2 March 1935, p. 8.

The Irish Press, 4 October 1934, p. 3.

Kerry Reporter, 21 July 1934, p. 12.

Miller, Meg, 'How Postage Stamps Are The Ultimate Design Challenge', Fast Company online, accessed 5 December 2021.

The Munster Express, 13 July 1934, p. 2.

Sunday Independent, 17 June 1934, p. 1.

39. Collectable Cigarette Card

Belfast News-Letter, 31 October 1925, p. 10.

Blum, Alan, 'A History of Tobacco Trading Cards: From 1880s Bath Beauties to 1990s Satire', *Tobacco and Health*, edited by Karen Slama (New York: Plenum Press, 1995), pp. 923–4 .

Broom, John, *A History of Cigarette and Trade Cards: The Magic Inside the Packet* (Barnsley: Pen and Sword, 2018).

Evening Herald, 2 January 1917, p. 2.

Irish Photo Archive online, 'C211 – 1963 Interiors of Liam Devlin and Sons Ltd. Dublin Sweet Factory at Cork Street', accessed 16 February 2022.

40. Mullingar Town Trophy

Evening Herald, 31 July 1936, p. 8.

Gordon Bowe, Nicola, 'Evocative and Symbolic Memorials and Trophies by Percy Oswald Reeves', *Irish Arts Review Yearbook* 16: 131–8 (2000).

Irish Independent, 26 September 1935, p. 14.

Meath Chronicle, 12 January 1935, p. 5.

Offaly Independent, 22 December 1934, p. 2.

Westmeath Examiner, 11 July 1992, p. 7.

41. Waterford GAA Calendar Poster

De La Salle Waterford online, 'College History', 5 August 2021.

Huang, Martha E., 'The Spectacle of Representation: Calendar Girls, the Gaze and the Atelier', *Transtext(e)s Transcultures* 2 (2009).

Slevin, Gerry, *Nenagh Guardian*, 3 February 2007.

42. Scissors used to open the Cusack Stand

Croke Park online, '1924–1933', accessed 26 July 2021.

Irish Independent, 17 August 1938, p. 11.

Irish Independent, 27 November 1935, p. 13.

Irish Independent, 5 August 1938, p. 13.

The Irish Press, 13 August 1938, p. 14.

The Irish Press, 20 August 1938, p. 12.

*Limerick Leade*r, 7 December 1935, p. 15.

Sunday Independent, 1 December 1935, p. 7.

43. 'Thunder and Lightning' Final Ticket

BBC.com, 'Chamberlain announces Britain is at war with Germany', accessed 2 January 2022.

Croke Park online, 'GAA Museum Primary Schools Resource Pack', accessed 28 June 2021.

Evening Echo, 4 September 1989, p. 6.

Harrington, John, *Evening Herald*, 9 September 2000, p. 109.

History.com, 'Britain and France Declare War on Germany', accessed 2 January 2022.

O'Hehir, Michael, *The Sunday Press*, 27 August 1978, p. 27.

Smith, Raymond, *Evening Herald*, 12 March 1976, p. 6.

The Southern Star, 2 September 1978, p. 24.

44. Football from All-Ireland Final

Evening Press, 14 March 1979, p. 29.

Hickey, J.D., *Irish Independent*, 11 January 1956, p. 10.

45. Unofficial Match Programme

Football Site online, 'Football Programme Miscellany', accessed 31 July 2021.

The Cork Examiner, 28 August 1944, p. 4.

The Nationalist and Leinster Times, 9 September 1944, p. 4.

46. Handball Medal found in South Africa

Connacht Tribune, 3 July 1954, p. 21.

Connacht Tribune, 25 August 1956, p. 3.

47. Napkin from Hotel Empire, New York

Brehany, Martin, '1947: The Fairytale in New York', Independent.ie, published 17 September 2010.

Fitzpatrick, Paul, *The Fairytale in New York: The Story of Cavan's Finest Hour* (Wicklow: Ballpoint Press, 2013).

The Irish Times online, 'New York Hosts Kerry and Cavan', published 2 December 2009.

Moran, Seán, 'From TB to Polio: GAA is No Stranger to Disease Disruptions', *The Irish Times* online, published 25 May 2020.

Rouse, Paul, 'A Bronx tale: How GAA took hold in New York', *Irish Examiner* online, 5 May 2017.

48. Player's Please Figure

Crompton, John L., 'Sponsorship of Sport by Tobacco and Alcohol Companies – A Review of the Issues', *Journal of Sport and Social Issues* 72: 148–67 (December 1993).

Donegal Democrat, 9 February 1979, p. 19.

The Cork Examiner, 21 May 1971, p. 5.

Irish Independent, 5 October 1974, p. 8.

The Irish Press, 9 May 1972, p. 20.

The Munster Express, 15 April 1977, p. 19.

Nottingham Museums online, 'Players Cigarette Advertising Archive', accessed 14 February 2022.

The Sligo Champion, 16 June 1972, p. 16.

Whitney, Seán, 'The Irish Tobacco Business 1779–1935', PhD Thesis University of Limerick (2019) .

49. Cap signed by Christy Ring

Irish Independent, 4 September 1953, p. 10.

Leitrim Leader, 13 September 1952, p. 3.

Limerick Leader, 13 September 1952, p. 10.

Veneti, Anastasia, Karadimitriou, Achilleas and Patsiaouras, Georgios, 'From autographs to fan-celebrity selfies: A new media genre in the evolving participatory media culture', LSE Media and Communications online, accessed 27 June 2021.

YouTube, 'Football 1950 & Hurling 1952', accessed 27 June 2021.

50. Gold Key from Opening of Casement Park

Casement Park online, 'About Casement', accessed 23 October 2021.

Irish Independent, 27 May 1953, p. 10.

Irish News online, 'Back in the day – How they fought the case for Casement', published 4 September 2019.

McClousland, Nelson, 'Casement Park needs a new name to signal new era for GAA', *Belfast Telegraph* online, published 10 December 2014.

51. Miniature Sam Maguire Cup

Belfast Telegraph, 22 September 2003, p. 28.

Irish Independent, 16 May 1978, p. 6.

The Irish Press, 30 September 1975, p. 13.

52. *Our Games* Annual

Anderson, David, 'Why Christmas annuals are still a favoured gift – 195 years after the first one was published', The Conversation online, published 24 December 2018.

Clare Local Studies Project, *The Celtic Times: Michael Cusack's Gaelic Games Newspaper 1887* (Clare: CLASP Press, 2003).

Coleman, Marie, 'Ó Caoimh, Pádraig (Paddy O'Keeffe)', Dictionary of Irish Biography, published October 2009.

The Celtic Times, Michael Cusack's Gaelic Games Newspaper, GAA Museum Archive, Ref. 1-900-545-144, accessed 21 February 2022.

The Nationalist, 20 December 1958, p. 16.

Tipperary Digital Studies online, 'The Gaelic Weekly incorporating *The Gaelic Sportsman* vol. I, no. 1. 17 March 1956', accessed 13 February 2022.

The Tuam Herald, 21 December 1963, p. 5.

53. Wembley Match Programme

BBC.com, 'History of the World: Section of Wembley Stadium', accessed 19 February 2022.

Connacht Sentinal, 20 May 1958, p. 3.

Connacht Tribune, 14 December 1957, p. 14.

Dunne, Mick, *The Irish Press*, 24 August 1957, p. 12.

Dunne, Mick, *The Irish Press*, 21 May 1958, p. 9.

Hickey, John D., *Irish Independent*, 27 May 1958, p. 12.

Irish Independent, 17 July 1957, p. 8.

London GAA online, 'London 125: Wembley at Whit', published 25 March 2021.

Sunday Independent, 25 May 1958, p. 4.

54. Hurl from Turloughmore's Six-in-a-row

Turloughmore GAA online, 'A Brief History', accessed 16 August 2021.

Walsh, Sean, *Tuam Herald*, 23 November 2016, p. 64.

55. Co. Down Hand-knitted Cardigan

Fisk, Anna, '"Stitch for stitch, you are remembering": Knitting and Crochet as Material Memorialization', *Material Religion* 15(5): 553–76 (2019).

Loughran, Neil, 'The boys of summer: Down's 1968 heroes recall glorious All-Ireland triumph 50 years on', *The Irish News* online, published 21 September 2018.

Maxim, Mary, 'About Mary Maxim', accessed 2 October 2021.

56. Referee's Whistle

ACME online, 'The ACME Thunderer', accessed 20 December 2021.

Cooney, Donal, 'Jimmy Hatton – Referee, Hurler, Footballer, County Selector (both codes)', Wicklow GAA online, 27 March 2019.

Irish Independent, 21 September 1966, p. 13.

Independent.ie, 'Former referee Jimmy is a true Wicklow GAA legend', published 27 October 2005.

The Irish Press, 17 July 1963, p. 13.

The Irish Press, 22 July 1963, p. 20.

57. All-Star Jersey

Irish Independent, 21 February 1964, p. 21.

The Irish Press, 17 March 1964, p. 1.

Nenagh Guardian, 2 December 2006, Section: Sport.

Moran, Seán, 'It was 50 years ago … remembering the first-ever GAA All Star awards', *The Irish Times* online, published 19 February 2021.

58. Antrim Camogie Dress

Belfast News-Letter, 31 August 1964, p. 1.

Belfast News-Letter, 18 August 1973, p. 7.

Corrigan, Vawn, *Irish Tweed: History, Tradition, Fashion* (Dublin: O'Brien Press, 2020).

Donegal Democrat, 6 June 1980, p. 4.

Evening Echo, 15 September 1967, p. 10.

The Irish Press, 11 October 1967, p. 13.

Jefferson-Buchanan, Rachael, 'Uniform discontent: how women athletes are taking control of their sporting outfits', The Conversation online, published 25 July 2021.

59. First GAA Helmet

Crowe, Dermot, 'Surgeon Urges GAA to Face Up to Eye Injuries', Independent.ie, accessed 22 June 2003.

The Irish Press, 22 April 1970, p. 20.

Puirseal, Padraig, *The Irish Press*, 28 February 1969, p. 13.

60. Harty Cup Plaque

The Anglo-Celt, 13 January 1917, p. 21.

The Freeman's Journal, 15 May 1917, p. 7.

Evening Echo, 26 October 1967, p. 8.

Kearney, Frank, *Connacht Tribune*, 12 January 2007, p. 8.

Limerick Leader, 11 March 1964, p. 21.

Limerick Leader, 28 June 2003, p. 27.

Limerick Leader, 11 February 1989, p. 7.

O'Saughnessy, John, *Limerick Leader*, 14 February 1998, p. 26.

Sunday Independent, 26 June 1938, p. 13.

The Nationalist, 10 October 1917, p. 8.

61. Chalice with Football Medals

Irish Independent, 8 November 1915, p. 7

Independent.ie, '125 Greatest Wexford Footballers', published 8 January 2010.

New Ross Standard, 25 March 1977, p. 6.

Ó Faolain, Sean, *With the Gaels of Wexford* (Enniscorthy: Echo Offices, 1955).

62. Letter from Fr Tom Scully to Offaly Footballers

Corrigan, Kevin, 'Fr Tom Scully made important contribution to Offaly football's golden era', *Offaly Express* online, published 10 April 2020.

Kelly, Justin, 'Offaly GAA mourns the passing of two-time All-Ireland winner', *Offaly Express* online, 26 January 2019.

Rouse, Paul, 'Belief central to Fr Tom Scully's sermon to the Faithful', *Irish Examiner* online, published 13 April 2020.

63. Handmade Model of GAA Pitch

Irish Independent, 18 October 1977, p. 13.

The Irish Times online, 'GAA & Revolution in Ireland 1913–1921', published 22 October 2015.

Nenagh Guardian, 28 January 1961, p. 5.

Nenagh Guardian, 26 February 1955, p. 2.

Nenagh Guardian, 2 August 1975, p. 8.

Nenagh Guardian, 15 August 1987, p. 11.

64. Scór Programme

GAA.ie, 'Derry Gowen – Ceannródaí agus Laoch Mór Scór' published 15 January 2019.

GAA.ie, 'Scór', accessed 20 December 2021.

The Cork Examiner, 14 February 1978, p. 10.

65. Kilmacud Sevens Winners Plaque

Evening Echo, 29 August 1973, p. 12.

Evening Herald, 2 August 1919, p. 6.

GAA.ie, 'Eugene McGee RIP', published 5 May 2019.

Gaelic Life, 19 September 2013, p. 14.

Gaelic Life, 20 September 2012, p. 28.

The Irish Press, 17 February 1971, p. 15.

The Irish Press, 15 August 1984, p. 13.

SD 7s online, 'West Coast Sevens', accessed 5 April 2022.

66. Joe Kernan's Runners-up Plaque

Foley, Cliona, 'Kernan uses 1916 medal to lift Armagh for final push', Independent.ie, published 24 September 2002.

Irish Examiner online, 'Loser's plaque gave Armagh spur for glory', published 23 September 2003.

MacKenna, Ewan and Oisín McConville, *The Gambler: Oisín McConville's Story* (Edinburgh: Mainstream Publishing, 2007).

Evening Herald, 29 August 2002, p. 79.

Harrington, John, 'Flashback: 2002 All-Ireland SFC Final – Armagh vs Kerry', GAA.ie, published 20 March 2020.

YouTube, '2002 All-Ireland Senior Football Final: Armagh v Kerry', uploaded 20 March 2020.

67. Dóirín Mhic Mhurchú's Handmade Press Pass

Browne, Donald R., 'Raidió na Gaeltachta: Reviver, Preserver or Swan Song for the Irish Language?', *European Journal of Communication* 7: 415–33 (1992).

Finn, Clodagh, 'Clodagh Finn: The first female sports reporter blazed a trail on her Honda 50', *Irish Examiner* online, published 6 April 2022.

'GAA bid to Boost Use of Irish', *Irish Examiner*, 24 September 1979, p. 1.

'All in a Day's Sport', *The Irish Press*, 8 March 1974, p. 11.

Murphy, John, 'Women's Lib in Waterford', *Irish Examiner*, 6 February 1979, p. 10.

Ó Ciardha, Mártan, Ainm, 'Mhic Mhurchú, Dóirín (1930–2014)', accessed 28 April 2022.

Ó Ciardha, Mártan, 'Céad Slán le Dóirín', Tuairisc.ie, published 7 December 2014.

RTÉ Archives, 'Raidió na Gaeltachta Begins Broadcasting, 1972', accessed 28 April 2022.

68. John Egan's Glove

Foley, Michael, *Kings of September: The Day Offaly Denied Kerry Five in a Row* (Dublin: O'Brien Press, 2007).

GAA.ie, 'Oral History: Seamus Aldridge', accessed 25 November 2021.

The Irish Press, 9 April 1982, p. 19.

Mackey, Liam, 'John Egan: The Corkman who only ever wanted to play for Kerry …', *Irish Examiner* online, published 31 August 2019.

69. Poc Fada Marking Stone

GAA.ie, 'Poc Fada', accessed 3 October 2021.

The Irish Press, 5 June 1970, p. 15.

McGarry, Marion, 'Why Whit Sunday is the unluckiest day of the year', RTÉ Brainstorm online, published 19 August 2021.

Sheridan, Kathy, 'Mighty Hurling Around the Mountain', *The Irish Times* online, published 16 August 2004.

70. Prison Art from Long Kesh

Flynn, M.K., 'Decision-making and Contested Heritage in Northern Ireland: The Former Maze Prison/Long Kesh', *Irish Political Studies* 26(3): 383–401 (2011).

The Irish Press, 22 January 1974, p. 4.

Prisons Memory Archive online, 'The H-Blocks', accessed 7 December 2021.

Reynolds, Mark, 'The Gaelic Athletic Association and the 1981 H-Block Hunger Strike', *The International Journal of the History of Sport* 34(3–4): 217–235 (2017).

Strabane Chronicle, 28 January 1984, p. 14.

71. *Up for the Final* Concert Programme

Cunningham, John, *Connacht Sentinel*, 7 September 1982, p. 8.

Irish Independent, 1 September 1982, p. 8.

Reilly, Terry, *Western People*, 22 September 1982, p. 13.

The Sligo Champion, 27 August 1982, p. 8.

Tipperary Star, 11 September 1982, p. 14.

72. Centenary Cairn

Conway, Michael, 'Handing of the Tradition – Kilclief Style', *Down GAA Yearbook 1984* (Down GAA: 1984).

Devlin, Michael, 'Pat Watterson's legacy lives on in Kilclief Ben Dearg GAC', GAA.ie, published 18 June 2019.

Manning, C., *Irish Field Monuments* (Dublin: Department of the Environment, Heritage and Local Government, 2004).

The Munster Express, 18 February 1983, p. 30.

Strangford Information online, 'Kilclief Ben Dearg GAC', accessed 19 February 2022.

73. 'Donegal Goes Home' Centennial Poster

Donegal Democrat, 15 March 1974, p. 8.
Donegal Democrat, 29 July 1983, p. 11.
Donegal Democrat, 10 August 1984, p. 12.
Donegal Democrat, 27 July 1984, p. 12.
Donegal News, 11 August 1984, pp. 8, 17.
Mary From Dungloe online, accessed 18 February 2022.

74. Sculpture Presented to Michael O'Hehir

Connolly, John and Paddy Dolan, 'Sport, media and the Gaelic Athletic Association: The quest for the "youth" of Ireland', *Media, Culture & Society* 34(4): 407–23 (2012).
Creedon, Seán, 'Remembering Micháel O'Hehir: Born 100 Years Ago', *Ireland's Own*, No. 5776, 21 August 2020.
GAA Museum online, 'All Star Posters', accessed 18 January 2022.
Rowan Gillespie online, 'About', accessed 17 January 2022.
Irish Independent, 6 February 1988, p. 5.
O'Brien, Peadar, *The Irish Press*, 26 February 1988, p. 14.
O'Hehir, Michael, *My Life and Times* (Dublin: Blackwater Press, 1996).
O'Hehir, Peter, *The Irish Press*, 26 February 1988, p. 14.
RTÉ Archives online, 'O'Hehir, Michael', accessed 17 January 2022.
YouTube, 'The 1988 Football and Hurling All Stars Awards Show', accessed 17 January 2022.

75. Trevor Giles's Sleeveless Jersey

Crane, Diane, *Fashion and Its Social Agendas: Class, Gender, and Identity in Clothing* (Chicago: University of Chicago Press, 2000).
Foley, Cliona, *Evening Herald*, 6 August 1999, p. 34.
RTÉ.ie, 'GAA permits sleeve sponsorship while Special Congress date set', published 18 September 2021.

76. Donegal Champions Jigsaw

Donegal Democrat, 4 March 1993, p. 23.
Persona Design online, 'GAA Stationary', accessed 4 April 2022.

77. 'Dancing at the Crossroads' Cassette

Doyle, Tom, *Set the Heather Blazing: A Graphic Novel of Wexford's 1996 Hurling All-Ireland* (Wexford: Yellow Belly, 2021).
The 42.ie, 'Dancing at the Crossroads 20 years on: the song that summed up a summer and toppled the Spice Girls', published 3 September 2016.

78. Colie K's Hole in the Ceiling

Harrington, John, 'Flashback – 1998 All-Ireland Football Final: Galway v Kildare', GAA.ie, accessed 25 August 2021.
Smith, Aaron C.T. and Bob Stewart, 'The Travelling Fan: Understanding the Mechanisms of Sport Fan Consumption in a Sport Tourism Setting', *Journal of Sport & Tourism* 12 (3–4): 155–81 (2011).
Weed, Mike, 'Exploring the sport spectator experience: virtual football spectatorship in the pub', *Soccer & Society* 9(2): 189–197 (2008).
YouTube, '1998 All-Ireland Senior Football Final: Galway vs Kildare', published 23 March 2020.

79. 'John 3:7' Sign

Bray, Allison, *Irish Independent*, 12 August 2009, p. 1.
Corbett, Peter, *Limerick Leader*, 11 February 2017, p. 3.
Corr, Aidan, *Limerick Leader*, 8 July 2000, p. 10.
Finnertan, Aoife, *Evening Herald*, 26 July 2006, p. 10.
Irish Examiner online, 'Limerick supporter famous for John 3:7 sign at GAA games dies', published 9 March 2020.
Ó Muircheartaigh, Joe, *Irish Examiner*, 11 March 2020, p. 7.
O'Regan, Donal, *Limerick Leader*, 11 March 2020, p. 11.
Raleigh, John, 'Frank Hogan, holder of "John 3:7" sign at GAA matches, dies aged 81', *The Irish Times* online, 9 March 2020.

Sunday Independent, 4 July 2010, p. 1.

YouTube, 'FULL VERSION 1987 – Cash vs Lendl – Wimbledon', uploaded 20 August 2021.

80. Shane Curran's Kicking Tee

Breheny, Martin, 'Canny Curran has tee total solution for kick-outs', Independent.ie, published 7 March 2006.

TG4, 'Shane Curran', *Laochra Gael*, broadcast 28 January 2022.

Curran, Shane, *Cake: The Autobiography of a Passionate, Outspoken Sportsman and Entrepreneur* (Dublin: Penguin, 2014).

Fogarty, John, 'Let goalkeepers tee it up', *Irish Examiner* online, published 2 May 2013.

Gaelic Life, 16 October 2009, p. 34.

Keys, Colm, 'Goalkeepers teed off over new rule change', Independent.ie, published 11 February 2005.

O'Connell, Cian, 'Gary Rogers: "The role a goalkeeper plays now is vitally important"', GAA.ie, published 23 March 2020.

O'Connell, Sandra, 'How I made it: Shane Curran', *The Sunday Times* online, published 22 May 2011.

Rosandich, T.J., 'Sports Equipment and Technology', *The Sport Journal* online, accessed 4 April 2022.

81. Anthony Tohill's Football Boots

Coleman, Eamonn with Maria McCourt, *The Boys of '93: Derry's All-Ireland Kings* (Dublin: Merrion Press, 2018).

Evening Herald, 16 February 1995, p. 97.

Footy Headlines online, '"25 Years Old" – Full Adidas Predator History – 1994–2020', accessed 15 October 2021.

Hennig, Ewald M. and Thorsten Sterzing, 'The influence of soccer shoe design on playing performance: a series of biomechanical studies', *Footwear Science* 2(1): 3–11 (2010).

Maddeaux, Sabrina, 'Why footwear has far more to do with identity and expression than mere function', *National Post* online, published 13 April 2018.

Sullivan, Arthur, 'Legends: Anthony Tohill', GAA.ie, published 26 May 2015.

82. Kit Manager's Bag

GAA.ie, 'GAA President's Awards for 2022 announced', published 10 February 2022.

Hess, Alex, 'An Ode to Kit Men: Soccer's Unheralded Heroes', Vice.com, published 11 March 2016.

McPeake, Dermot, 'The Kit Man', Derry GAA.ie, accessed 23 September 2021.

83. Signed Armagh Ladies Football Jersey

Belfast News-Letter, 21 October 2013, p. 24.

Bogue, Declan, '"Football is for everyone": How Armagh ladies' new facilities will blaze a trail for future generations', *Belfast Telegraph* online, published 18 May 2020.

McKenna, Michael, 'Armagh Ladies GAA get thumbs-up to build exciting new community centre and sports pavilion 'home', Armaghi.com, 21 December 2019.

O'Kane, Cahair, '"I wasn't pioneering, I just wanted to play" – Caroline O'Hanlon on her incredible sporting career', *Irish News* online, published 26 January 2019.

Pepper, Diarmuid, 'Scary but exciting times ahead for Armagh ladies footballers', *Irish News* online, published 20 July 2019.

RTÉ.ie, 'No place like home – Armagh women's struggle for a level playing pitch', accessed 16 November 2021, published 1 February 2021.

World Netball online, 'Northern Ireland', accessed 2 January 2022.

84. Waterford Crystal Chandelier

Kane, Conor, 'Waterford Crystal: how cracks appeared in the recession', *The Irish Times* online, 14 December 2014.

The Munster Express, 23 December 1994, p. 18.

85. *Gaelic Games: Football* PlayStation 2 Game

Keys, Colm, 'Top Names Missing from Computer Game', Independent.ie, published 30 September 2005.

The Journal.ie, 'This is the inside story behind the Gaelic Football and Hurling games on the Playstation – Part 1', published 19 September 2015.

The Journal.ie, 'This is the story behind *those* Gaelic Football and Hurling games – Part 2', published 20 September 2015.

86. Tyrone 'GAA 125' Anniversary Jersey

Gaelic Life, 27 March 2009, p. 1.

YouTube. '2009 Dublin vs Tyrone Croke Park', uploaded 1 May 2020.

87. Brian Cody's Cap

Bass-Kreuger, Maude, 'Everything to know about the history of the baseball cap', Vogue.com, published 28 May 2019.

Kilkenny People online, 'Brian Cody keen to push on after he extends stay with Kilkenny', published 16 January 2021.

Lingan, John, 'How the Baseball Cap Went From Athletic Gear to Fashion Statement', *Smithsonian Magazine* online, published April 2020.

McDowell, Colin, *Hats: Status, Style and Glamour* (London: Thames and Hudson, 1992).

This Basketball World online, 'A Comprehensive History of Basketball Uniforms', published 8 October 2020.

88. Flag Trolley

Croke Park online, 'Stewards', accessed 25 February 2022.

Evening Echo, 4 May 1966, p. 8.

GAA.ie, *Gaelic Athletic Association Official Rules Part 2*, accessed 3 April 2022.

Leinster Express, 14 August 1999, p. 51.

89. GAA Congress Voting Card

Brophy, Shane, *Nenagh Guardian*, 24 April 2010, p. 22.

Campbell, John, *Sunday Life*, 13 December 2009, p. 95.

Canty, Brian, *Irish Examiner*, 29 November 2010, p. 25.

GAA Learning online, 'GAA Go Games', accessed 25 February 2022.

GAA.ie, 'GAA Structures', accessed 25 February 2022.

GAA.ie, 'Timeline 1945–2015', published 8 December 2015.

Irish Examiner online, 'GPA Officially Recognised by GAA', published 17 April 2010.

Moore, Cormac, *The GAA V Douglas Hyde: The Removal of Ireland's First President as GAA Patron* (Cork: Collins Press, 2012).

90. Hawk-Eye Camera

Collins, H. and R. Evans, 'Sport-decision aids and the "CSI-effect": Why cricket uses Hawk-Eye well and tennis uses it badly', *Public Understanding of Science* 21(8): 904–21 (2012).

Deegan, Gordon, *Evening Herald*, 3 December 2013, p. 19.

Fogarty, John, 'HawkEye's presence in Championship 2020 hangs in balance', *Irish Examiner* online, published 22 September 2020.

Hawk-Eye online, 'Hawk-Eye in GAA', accessed 28 November 2021.

McIntyre, John, *Connacht Sentinel*, 20 August 2013, p. 32.

Sweeney, Peter, 'Hawk-Eye say that controversial All-Ireland final call was correct', RTÉ.ie, published 20 August 2019.

91. Rubber Bas Hurl

Connaught Telegraph, 5 November 2013, Section: Sport.

Cormican, Eoghan, *Irish Examiner*, 1 January 2020, p. 8.

Dwyer, Ciara, 'Pat Carty – captain of the Irish Wheelchair Hurling team: "He said, 'you can't stand or walk', but I got the highest price for my cattle"', Independent.ie, published 28 June 2020.

European Parliament online, 'Creating opportunities in sport for people with disabilities', accessed 24 February 2022.

GAA.ie, 'Diversity and Inclusion', accessed 24 February 2022.

GAA.ie, 'Interprovincial Wheelchair Hurling a first step to Paralympics', published 8 October 2013.

GAA.ie, 'The Rules of Wheelchair Hurling', accessed 24 February 2022.

GAA.ie, 'Wheelchair Hurling Given the Thumbs Up', published 22 November 2013.

Martin, John, *Gaelic Life*, 1 May 2014, p. 27.

Sligo Champion, 4 November 2014, p. 53.

92. Fundraising Wall

Leitrim GAA online, *Programme for the Official Opening of McGovern Aughavas Leitrim GAA Centre of Excellence*, 7 October 2019.

Magnier, Eileen, 'Bricks in the Wall Cement Leitrim Connections Around the World', RTÉ.ie, published 26 March 2019.

Ó Buacháin, Déaglán, 'McGovern Aughavas Leitrim GAA Centre of Excellence', *Leitrim Guardian* 2021 (53): 122–5 (2021).

93. Artane Band Tunic

Artane Band online, 'Artane Band History', accessed 2 October 2021.

Irish Independent, 18 March 1969, p. 12.

94. Five-in-a-row Manhole Cover

Dublin City Council online, 'Dublin City Coat of Arms', accessed 24 July 2021.

Dublin GAA online, 'History of Crest', accessed 5 August 2021.

English, Michael, *The Three Castles of Dublin: An Eclectic History of Dublin Through the Evolution of the City's Coat of Arms* (Dublin: Four Courts Press, 2016).

95. *Transilience* by David Sweeney

GAA Museum and Fighting Words, *Close to Croke Park* (Dublin: GAA Museum and Fighting Words, 2021).

Croke Park online, 'About Transilience', accessed 18 February 2022.

Dolan, Anne, 'Killing and Bloody Sunday, November 1920' in *The Historical Journal* 49(3): 789–810 (September 2006).

Moran, Seán, 'Fabric of time: How a former Dublin hurler created a haunting image of Croke Park', *The Irish Times* online, published 21 August 2020.

96. Cúl Camps Backpack

Devlin, Michael, 'Wexford host first ever Kellogg's GAA Cúl Camp for Autistic children', GAA.ie, published 13 August 2019.

VHI.ie, 'VHI Press Releases', accessed 27 July 2021.

97. All-Ireland Final Yellow Sliotar

Fogarty, John, 'Yellow sliotar to be used for all inter-county games going forward', *Irish Examiner* online, 17 January 2021.

Harrington, John, 'The science behind the yellow sliotar', GAA.ie, published 16 October 2020.

Moran, Kieran, 'The Story Behind Hurling's New Yellow Sliotar', RTÉ Brainstorm online, published 12 October 2020.

98. Gaeil Ruairí Óg Mural

Ruairí Óg online, 'Ruairis Open Laochra Gael Mural', accessed 5 April 2022.

99. Maggie Farrelly's Referee Report Card

Crowe, Dermot, *Leinster Express*, 4 March 1989, p. 30.

Drogheda Independent, 23 May 1980, p. 23.

GAA.ie, 'Maggie Farrelly to referee Cavan SFC Final replay', published 8 November 2021.

Hietala, Brett and James G. Archibald, 'Barriers to Female Officials in Sports', ACPA online, accessed 25 February 2022.

Keys, Colm, Independent.ie, 'Mould-breaker Maggie Farrelly named on referees' panel for National League', published 28 January 2022.

Lynott, Laura, '"The ultimate goal": Maggie Farrelly on being the first woman to referee at a senior men's county final', Independent.ie, published 9 November 2021.

Westmeath Examiner, 24 March 1990, p. 21.

100. Sculpture of Richard 'Droog' Walsh by Seamus Connolly

Bartley, Colin, 'Triple All-Ireland Winning Captain to be Immortalised in Bronze', Kilkenny*Now*.ie, published 28 October 2020.

de Búrca, Marcus, 'Walsh, Richard ("Droog")', Dictionary of Irish Biography, published October 2009.

The Irish Press, 1 December 1965, p. 13.

Raschke, Wendy J., 'Athletic Images and the Monumentalization of Victory', *The Oxford Handbook of Sport and Spectacle in the Ancient World*, edited by Thomas F. Scanlon and Alison Futrell (2021).

RTÉ.ie, 'Mary McAleese Unveils Dermot Earley Statue', published 27 August 2011.

Seamus Connolly online, accessed 18 February 2022.

Spory, Michael, 'Looking Back, Standing Still, Moving Forward: Monument, Stadium, and Social Narrative in Contemporary South Africa', *Athanor* 32: 111–9 (2014).

Walsh, Eoin, 'New statue brings to life a Kilkenny hurler whose legacy defines early golden era', *Kilkenny People* online, published 13 October 2021.

Index

D

Dalton, John (Archbishop) 182
Daly, Michael 139
Darby, Seamus 148
Davin, Maurice 25, 31
Davitt, Michael 28
de Valera, Éamon 3
Delea, Kate 87
Denman Dean, John 128
Denvir, James 156
Derry 55, 175, 176, 192
Dillon, John 28
Dineen, Frank Brazil 44, 52
Dingle 2
Donegal 159, 164
Donnellan, John 127
Donnellan, Michael 127
Donnellan, Pat 7, 127
Dowling, John 91, 124
Down 63, 119, 123, 152, 156, 175, 193
Doyle, Aidan 135
Doyle, John Joe 76
Drogheda 31
Drumcondra 160
Dublin 4, 5, 6, 15, 19, 27, 39, 47, 56, 60, 75, 89, 91, 93, 95, 97, 99, 103, 109, 111, 115, 124, 127, 128, 131, 136, 139, 143, 144, 148, 155, 160, 183, 184, 195, 199, 200, 203
Duke, P.J. 107
Dún Laoghaire-Rathdown 200
Dunboyne 211
Dungarvan 72
Dunmanaway 67

E

Earley, Dermot 212
Egan, John 148
Emmet, Robert 27
England 76

Ennis 1, 39, 132
Etchingham, Sean 23

F

Fagan, George 43
Farrelly, Maggie 211
Feakle 1
Ferguson, Des 'Snitchy' 111
Fermanagh 83, 95, 112, 140, 211
Fermoy 87
Festubert 51
Fitzgerald, Dick 48
Fitzgerald, John 32
Flaherty, Jimmy 124
Flanagan, Paddy 8
Flynn, Tommy 5
Foley, William 23
Fraher, Dan 72
France 5, 51, 99
Frongoch 43, 49

G

Galway 3, 7, 19, 20, 58, 72, 75, 76, 91, 96, 104, 112, 119, 120, 127, 160, 167, 168, 171, 175, 192
Gannon, Joe 211
Gannon, Mary 211
George's Dock 200
Germany 91, 99
Giles, Trevor 163
Gillespie, Rowan 160
Gilmartin, Liam 100
Gladstone, William E. 28
Glenbeigh 32
Glenurquhart 51
Gortaganny 212
Gowen, Derry 140
Graiguecullen 64
Greece 68
Grimes, Éamonn 132
Gweedore 159

H

Harty, John (Archbishop) 132
Hatton, Jimmy 124
Haughney, Denis 'Buller' 64
Hayes, John 'Hotpoint' 176
Herne Hill 119
Higgins, John J. 52
Hitler, Adolf 99
Hogan, Frank 171
Hogan, Michael 60, 203
Hogan, Willie 64
Honan, Tony 39
Hoope, Thomas Alphonsus (Brother) 199
Horgan, Dinny 'Stonewall' 36
Horgan, Michael 36
Hugginstown 11
Humphreys, Sighle 59
Hunt, Tom 143
Hyde, Douglas 191

I

Inverness 51
Isle of Man 156

J

Jones' Road 44, 72
Jones, Tom (Fr) 32
Joyce, Pádraic 168

K

K., Colie 168
Kearney, Con 1
Keating, Seán 75
Kelly, Edward (Rev. Fr) 104
Kenny, Enda 79
Kenny, Henry 79
Kenny, Henry Junior 79
Kenny, Thomas J. 70
Keogh, Tommy 132
Kernan, Joe 144